TIPS FOR SUCCESSFUL LIVING

TIPS FOR SUCCESSFUL LIVING

NEIL and
MARGARET RAU

Crossland
BOOKS

TIPS FOR SUCCESSFUL LIVING
81-8408-122-7

Second Indiana Edition: 2008

Published by:
INDIANA PUBLISHING HOUSE
For
Cross land BOOKS
2/13 Ansari Road, Darya Ganj,
New Delhi-110 002

Printed by:
Saurabh Printers Pvt. Ltd.
INDIA

CONTESTS

one

What This Book Is About

> " All the world's a stage,
> And all the men and women merely players.
> They have their exits and their entrances;
> And one man in his time plays many parts. . ."
> --Shakespeare

YOU AND YOUR ROLE

FROM the moment you open your eyes in the morning until you close them at night you're on stage. Whether you realize it or not you are playing a role every day as surely as the actor of stage, screen or television.

The question is: Are you playing the part of the person you really want to be? Are you a star performer or a clown? Are you stepping on your own lines and falling flat on your face, or are you carrying off the affairs of the day with a flair?

Who is to judge you ? The professional actor has drama critics to draw him up short whenever he lays an egg. The people who **should** be your critics, your friends, are the very ones usually who keep quitest. The critic you can really trust is **yourself.**

BE YOUR OWN JUDGE

Try sitting down alone some night and honestly asking yourself how you are playing your role on the stage of life.

Look back over the day. Are you genuinely pleased with the performance you put on at home and in the office? Go beyond the day to the week, the month, the year. Does it all look good to you?

As for the role itself—do you like it? Are you playing a part that you feel suits you? Or are you just doing something to "earn a living"?

Go back farther to the dreams of your youthful years. Are you fulfilling them? Have you perhaps achieved something even more wonderful than those envisioned dreams? Or are you just dragging along from day to day, making do because Fate or Family or Responsibilities do not "allow" you to lead the interesting life you once imagined for yourself?

If this is what you've been doing, this book is for you. It promises you nothing that isn't yours already for the taking—a full, satisfying and successful life in which you, as the star performer, are playing your role with authority and self-confidence.

How do we know you can become such a star performer? Simply because we, the authors, have seen it done every day during our thirty-year-long intimate association with the stage and screen in Hollywood, New York and London. We have seen gauche new performers changed into polished entertainers who became great box-office draws and eventual winners of Oscars.

We have seen this happen through the development of certain techniques that these beginners were taught, either in acting schools or by foremost drama coaches.

YOU, TOO, CAN LEARN THESE TECHNIQUES

It occurred to the authors that millions of people would be interested in having the opportunity to follow these techniques in order to bring out their personalities and enrich their lives. So we collected methods, techniques, ideas and gimmicks from famous Hollywood drama coaches and their equally famous pupils. The techniques of such stars as Cary Grant, Doris Day, Rex Harrison, Burt Lancaster, Celeste Holm, Anne Bancroft, Elsa Lanchester, and the late Gary Cooper are included here. We've put together their various professional tips in this book to serve as your manual of instruction.

THE TECHNIQUES WORK

The techniques work, no matter who applies them, as other members of the film industry have discovered. Directors use them to get across to their players the manner in which they want scenes portrayed. Producers use them to persuade reluctant stars to accept roles they may want to reject.

Ross Hunter, producer-director of such successes as **Pillow Talk, Flower Drum Song and Imitation of Life**, admits to a frequent use of acting techniques to help him overcome crises.

Hunter considered Lana Turner perfect for the role of Lora Meredith in his new film Imitation of Life. But Lana had just emerged from the sensational Johnny Stompanato tragedy, which had made glaring headlines around the world. She was convinced the public would not accept her in a sympathetic role and was astonished that Hunter would even suggest her for the picture. She turned down his offer.

But Hunter wouldn't give up. Lana was right for the part, and he felt it would bring her out of her shell. So he made a date to go to Lana's home at ten o'clock one morning to discuss it.

Lana couldn't turn down Hunter's request because of his respected position, but she made it plain that nothing would change her mind.

Hunter, however, didn't intend to take no for an answer. On the appointed day he got up several hours before schedule and planted himself before his mirror. He rehearsed the screenplay from beginning to end. Then he went over to Lana's house.

From ten in the morning until six in the evening Hunter enacted the drama over and over for Lana, doing all the parts in turn, laughing, crying, even flinging himself on the imaginary coffin of the dead Negro mother, Annie Johnson. At last Lana was caught up in the spirit of the play. She accepted the role and the film was made.

Subsequently, there was another crisis. Hunter wanted Lana to make public appearances with the picture, but once more the bogey public reaction held her back. Hunter realized he couldn't convince her without the use of dramatics. So he invited her to his office.

The minute Lana entered, her eyes fell on a luxurious heap of expensive furs—sables, minks, chinchillas, which Hunter had borrowed for the occasion, along with a collection of diamond bracelets, necklaces and earrings.

He persuaded the star to model the furs and the diamonds while he sat back and, in the role of the public, enthusiastically admired her glamor. His acting convinced her. She went on the road and proved a great success.

ACTING IS GOING ON ALL AROUND YOU

Of course, you won't have to persuade Lana Turner to do anything for you. But it may be that by using Ross Hunter techniques you will be able to persuade someone of the value of an idea, the advantage of employing you, or the usefulness of a product you're trying to sell

Many people employ some of these techniques intuitively with great success. The lawyer who stirs the jury and the doctor whose bedside manner gains the confidence of his patient are both using acting techniques.

The same is true of the housewife who conducts an interesting PTA meeting a successfully brings off a dinner in honour of her husband's employer. The man who can hold your attention with the story he is telling, or get you to buy something you don't really want or need is doing the same thing.

DRAMA IS USED IN EVERYDAY LIFE, TOO

Some people even arrange little dramas to accomplish their end. Has this, for instance, ever happened to you? You go into a dress shop and try on a dress. Despite the saleslady's enthusiastic approval you aren't sold.

Then a second saleslady comes up and warmly admires your appearance. Because she obviously has nothing to gain by the sale you are convinced of the sincerity of her praise and buy the dress.

You never dream as you go out with your purchase that it was probably all prearranged by the salesladies, who had hit upon this method of helping one another "sell" uncertain prospects. It was probably a right purchase for you, but the second saleslady's "act" helped you make up your mind.

Ramiro, the Columbia Studio barber, told us about a customer sent to him by one of his long-time patrons. The man came in skeptically. No barber, hse said, had ever given him a satisfactory haircut.

Ramiro saw at once what the problem was. The man was parting his hair down the center. Ramiro had to use all his eloquence to persuade his new customer to allow him to change the part.Then without giving his customer a chance to find fault with the new style, Ramiro stood back and heartily admired his own handiwork.

"Why, it's altered your whole appearance," he exclaimed. "You look ten years younger."

The customer was impressed but still uncertain. After all, he had always worn his hair parted down the middle. The imaginative barber realized this, and as soon as his customer had left he carried his drama a little further. He telephoned the patron who had recommended the man.

"When you see your friend", he said, "don't comment on his haircut. Just tell him how good he looks today."

The friend complied, with the result that Ramiro acquired another permanent patron. It wasn't actually the haircut that brought back the customer but the barber's dramatization of the genuine improvement in his appearance.

HOW ARE YOU PLAYING YOUR SCENES?

How many times have you said, "If only I'd handled the situation properly I'd have come out on top."

Handling the situation properly is simply setting up your own scene and playing your role in it authoritatively. By using acting techniques you can do this with surety and at the same time enjoy the sense of confidence that comes with a good performance.

A few people already realize the importance of acting in their profession and make a point of boning up on the more important techniques. Salesmen, for instance, often take refresher courses in the latest selling methods.

The head of one of London's foremost beauty salons told us that the hairdressers hired for that establishment must undergo a long apprenticeship before their applications are even considered.

"You can learn how to set hair in six months," he explained. "But more important to us is the training of the personality so that the hairdresser will be adept at meeting and handling the public. This is the more difficult accomplishment and so it takes longer."

One young minister we know annually took a course in acting.

"I told myself that if these techniques enable actors to get across their secular messages so successfully, I certainly could make use of them to get over my far more important message of the love and goodness of God," he explained.

YOU, TOO, HAVE ACTING TALENT

What the people mentioned above do to display themselves more effectively to the world, you too can learn. In fact, you can go much further in preparing yourself for a fuller and more satisfying life by following the professional secrets given in this book. You cannot help being successful if you apply them, for one simple reason—**you, whoever you are or whatever your work, have real acting talent yourself.**

You do indeed, because acting is an instinct that all of us possess. Life is truly lived only in terms of the dramatic. This fact has been recognized from ancient times. Drama is the means by which the human race has been spurred forward.The war and fertility dances of primitive peoples, for instance, were a form of drama used as a means of whipping up enthusiasm for their goals. Ritualistic religious services were used to rally energy to accomplish difficult tasks at hand.

Today we employ a form of drama for the important occasions of life-weddings, graduation exercises, funeral services, dedication ceremonies. With what attention the stage is set for these performances! Music is chosen with great care. Elaborate stage props, including candles and impressive floral arrangements, provide a suitable setting for the actors who are to put on the "show,"

When these actors don't measure up to the grandeur of the setting in which they are placed, when the minister, rabbi or priest officiating at the wedding is perfunctory, the speaker for the graduation exercises pompous, the deliverer of the funeral oration dripping with trite sentimentality, how cheated we feel! This is because it's human nature to expert good acting daily in life as well as in the theatre.

YOU WERE ONCE A FINE ACTOR

As a baby nobody could surpass you in acting. You knew instinctively what to do in order to get what you wanted. As you grew older you played realistic games by yourself or with your playmates. You created little dramas, too, to call attention to yourself.

You were eminently successful because you performed naturally and with great self assurance. This confidence in yourself was what gave your childhood days so much vitality and zest.

What happened to you as you grew up?

A hundred and one restrictions sprang up around you like a hedge of thorns to choke your natural spontaneity. The harsh rules of an adult world destroyed your faith in your creative powers. By the time you reached adulthood you were probably already safely established in a rut.

But ruts don't make for happiness.

WHAT CAN YOU DO ABOUT IT NOW?

Take a fresh look at yourself. Ask yourself if life has given you all you deserve or are capable of. Ask yourself if it's really true that you haven't had the "breaks," that you don't have the talent, that it's a matter of fate.

Or is it just a matter of playing your role poorly? Most of us are capable of far more success and fulfillment in life than has actually come to us.

It is as though a man living in a squalid tenement room were within easy reach of a treasure horde which lies concealed under a loose plank in the floor. But since he knows nothing about such a treasure, it never occurs to him to search for it.

ACTORS ARE PEOPLE WHO HAVE CLAIMED THEIR TREASURE

Look at your favorite stage, screen or television personality with new eyes Remind yourself that he was once a person like you with flaws to overcome and inadequacies to correct.

What is the main difference between this actor and you? Not his engaging personality, or his acting ability, or his magnetic authority, but a wholehearted belief in himself. Some people call it egotism. Whatever it is, an actor cannot function without it.

You as an actor on the stage of life can't function, either unless you respect yourself.

Once you begin to respect yourself as someone with a unique and interesting personality and an important role to play in life, you will realize that personality is worth developing. You will want to do it.

ONE IMPORTANT RULE

There is one important rule in this venture that you should faithfully obey. Follow the directions and exercises we give you in the same spirit of fun that animated your childhood games. Acting is, after all, one of the few delightful professions in which you can actually play while you learn. If you don't believe us, drop in on any class of young drama students. The enthusiasm, good nature and camaraderie you find are electrifying.

Make this motto yours: "Don't take your work seriously; turn your work into play and take your play seriously." Then you'll find your treasure. And when you find it, we'll guarantee further that you'll leave your worries behind and come into fresh and invigorating new atmosphere.

If you're wise you'll use your newfound wealth to raise a mansion for your soul. You will be able not only to keep that mansion in order, but also to enlarge it and expand its grounds. This will be possible because you will have trained your servants—those native attributes and talents we all possess—to obey your voice and do your bidding.

two

Observation

OBSERVATION: MAGIC KEY NUMBER ONE

OBSERVATION is the first magic key toward playing your role for a successful and fuller life. It will open doors for you. It will renew for you all the excitement of living you felt as a child when the world was fresh and there was a new discovery to be made around every corner.

Observation is an age-old instinct. That's why children are so gifted with it. But modern adult man has allowed it to deteriorate. Too many of us are confined in humdrum ruts which we've worn so deep that we can no longer see over the top. No ,wonder we don't feel alive.

THE FIRST TOOL OF THE MODERN ACTOR

The Russian actor-producer-director Constantin Stanislavski, born in 1863, might be called the father of modern acting. He was the first to realize the importance of observation to the world of drama. For forty years in his Moscow Art Theatre he worked to eliminate all the cliches that were the standard trademark of the actor. Out went all the simpering romantic guff, the angry gnashing of teeth, the grief-stricken wringing of hands.

The first thing he taught his young actors was to throw away the textbooks, go out into the street and observe life at first hand.

Major drama coaches of the stage and the motion picture industry still teach their students this beginner's dictum. It is followed faithfully by all successful actors and actresses. The polished performance you see on stage, screen or television doesn't come from a bag of tricks. It comes from a thorough study of the personality the actor wants to portray, as well as the milieu in which that personalitsy moves.

HOW PLAYERS CASE THEIR ROLES

"I spent two months working with deaf and blind children at institutes in New York and Chicago before I felt I was ready to rehearse **The Miracle Worker,"** Anne Bancroft told us. "I also studied Annie Sullivan herself until I became so familiar with her attitudes toward life that I felt I could step into her shoes."

Dolores Hart said that she could never have feelingly portrayed the title role of the tormented Jewish girl in the motion picture **Lisa** without having first spent long sessions with a young Jewish emigrant who had herself suffered the horrifying experiences of concentration camp life.

HOW ABOUT YOU?

Have you made a careful study of yourself to correct the flaws and enhance the good points in your personality,. so you can present a positive and dynamic front to the world?

Have you studied the milieu in which you move? Have you, in fact, made yourself so aware of it that you can use it to your advantage in your present job, or as a base from which to climb to something better?

It will pay you to become more alert to yourself and to your surroundings. Remember—that is as necessary toward playing your role properly as it is to the professional actors and actresses.

ONE STEP FURTHER

An experienced actor has learned, however, not to wait for a role before he starts to observe life. His job requires a full-time observation. Little nuances of feeling or unique gestures or facial expressions which he can drop into his knapsack of memory may turn out to be the treasure he needs for a future performance.

"We actors aren't artists," Willian Holden confided to the authors one afternoon on location in Hamburg, Germany, where we were covering his movie, **The Counterfeit Traitor.** "We're interpreters." And he quoted director John Houston's appraisal: "Actors are thieves going from village to village stealing pigs."

"But there's a certain honor among thieves," the realistic, hard-hitting Holden elaborated. "And if with his stolen pigs an actor can stir an audience to think above and beyond their ordinary lives, he feels his thefts are worthwhile."

ARE YOU A TRAINED OBSERVER?

Are you a trained observer? The answer is yes, at least in the field you have chosen, if you happen to be a member of the legal, medical or scientific professions. Your powers of observation are perhaps more general if you are an author or artist. However, in no other field is observation so thorough as in the field of criminology. Without that power of observation on which the detective relies there would be many less criminals behind bars today.

The following illustration taken from the early nineteenth century will demonstrate how an observant eye can prevent crime.

One day Vidocq, one of France's most colorful detectives, happened to glance at a figure leaving the Pavillon de Flore in Paris. This highly respectable-looking gentleman was known to everyone as the Marquis de Chambreuil, chief of the palace police. His chest was covered with decorations to prove his rank and his martial accomplishments.

But Vidocq's observant eyes passed from the impeccable attire and imposing carriage to the man's face. He arrested the fellow at once. For he was the notorious escaped convict Chambreuil, who had taken advantage of Louis XVIII's pity for indigent aristocrats to palm himself off as one. He had managed so to ingratiate himself in the royal favor that he had been appointed to a position of responsibility and honor. He would no doubt have succeeded in his plan of robbing the king if not for Vidocq's trained powers of observation.

The art of criminology has progressed far since Vidocq's time. Today, laboratory work can reconstruct the appearance of a criminal and even hazard a guess as to his profession simply by analyzing microscopic substances found at the scene of the crime. But it remains for the eye of the trained observer to do the valuable research in detective work. This is so true that today all great government agencies from Scotland Yard to the FBI concentrate on training their men in the art of observing even the most minute details of any scene in which they may find themselves.

OBSERVATION AND YOU

You needn't be a detective to profit by training in observation. The woman who notices a man's tie and later makes a point of commenting on it will impress him favorably. 'The salesman who takes note of a golf trophy on the wall of a prospect can often make a sale by discussing the game the next time he meets his prospective client.

The hotel proprietor who notes the habits and idiosyncracies of his guests and caters to them can always be sure of a full house. The waiter or waitress who is observant of the patrons' special wants painlessly increases the size of tips.

This practice of observation even in small matters can lead to advancement in any occupation, for it always gives the impression of alertness and interests in others. More than this, you will feel an increased sense of confidence that may add up eventually to a really big achievement.

WHAT KIND OF OBSERVER ARE YOU?

If you consider yourself a pretty good observer, start asking yourself questions.

What color is my wife's hair? What color are her eyes? What dress was she wearing last evening?

What tie was my husband wearing yesterday? What color were his shoes? Did he wear a shirt that required cuff links?

If you can answer these question, go farther afield. Can you, for instance, describe accurately a friend's living room or your office? Can you evoke in your mind's eye the appearance of employees with whom you work every day—or state accurately the color of their hair or eyes?

Can you describe in detail the streets you pass along on the way to work? Can you name points of interest that have attracted your glance? Unusual flowers or trees or shrubs, or even people you might meet?

If an accident or crime were to occur before your eyes and arrest your attention automatically, would you afterwards be able to describe that event in accurate detail?

Our son, Robert Rau, who spent a year as a prosecuting attorney in the Los Angeles City Courts, tell us that the discrepancies in the descriptions of witnesses often make it almost impossible to arrive at the truth. This is because most of us are untrained in observation. We reduce everything to a blur because our minds are myopically focused on some personal problem or situation. Many of us come to work tired, distracted and irritable because we refuse to let go. Yet it is the ability to let go occasionally, by focusing on the outside world, that brings new perspective and energy to the problems of the day.

DON'T WAIT FOR THE BIG EVENT

Do you have to wait until you take a trip before you really start to observe? This is a normal practice with most people.

John W. Gardner, president of the Carnegie Fcundation and recipient of the Medal of Freedom, the highest honor the President of our country can bestow, says in his book, **Self Renewal,** "Travel shakes us out of our apathy, and we regain an attentiveness that heightens every experience. The exhilaration of travel has many sources, but surely one of them is that we recapture in some measure the unspoiled awareness of children."

When you understand this, you can travel in a foreign city without ever leaving your own home. All you need do is to tell yourself that the place where you are living is foreign to visitors from elsewhere. Can you tell those visitors that you have seen the points of interest in which they are so vitally interested?

When the authors were in England for their first trip they were escorted around London by John Willis, a public relations man who had undertaken to show them the city.

"I've never been here before," the young man confessed rather sheepishly at the House of Parliament. At the Tower of London he commented wonderingly, "I used to play here all the time as a child. I haven't been back since."

When we thanked him for his services as our guide, he thanked us in turn for helping him see his birthplace more clearly.

Don't confine your sightseeing to the places recommended by your local chamber of commerce. Start looking for interesting items in the everyday aspects of your city. Remember, objects that you have been taking for granted would be fascinating adventures to foreigners—the escalator, the elevator, the subway, to mention a few. Try to experience them through new eyes.

BE AN EXPLORER AT NO EXPENSE

You can see a strange city without leaving home and you can be an explorer without traveling to distant wilds. Just take a second look at your back yard or the nearby park. By judicious observation you will find there wonders as great as any on earth.

Jean Henri Fabre, the celebrated entomologist, born in 1823, in the French village of St. Leon, Aveyron, was so poor he could not afford to attend the university. He became a schoolteacher in the native province. He married and fathered seven children. His parents could not support themselves and came to live with him, too. His meager salary was insufficient to care for them all, so he had to fill most of his free time with private tutoring, reviewing and other odd jobs.

Fabre lacked the educational opportunities that other great naturalists of his day enjoyed, but he worked diligently to compensate for this lack by teaching himself physics, chemistry and mathematics. He spent his scant spare time on his hobby—the study of insect life.

Fabre discovered facts as amazing about these sunparched denizens of the stony meadows of Provencal as his fellow explorers were finding in the most remote jungles of the world. Today his beautifully written biographies of wasps and glow worms, cicadas and beetles hold a special place in the literature of natural history. No doubt his deep absorption in the world around him led to his long life span of ninety-two years.

HOW TO GATHER TREASURES FOR YOUR KNAPSACK

Why not, like Fabre, search for something interesting even in the commonplace objects around you? Such observations as these have been responsible for many of the world's most useful inventions and opened up new vistas to mankind in general.

By taking note of how a ship disappeared over the horizon, Columbus deduced that the earth was round and set his sails westward to discover two new continents. An apple falling to the ground woke Isaac Newton to the law of gravity. Eli Whitney evolved the principle of the steam engine simply by watching a kettle boil.

Open your eyes and you will become aware of amazing sights in your own vicinity. Don't be afraid to ask questions. Ask the gardener, the maintenance man, the elevator boy, the garbage collector. You will be surprised at how much you will learn. You may discover that people you have been taking for granted are interesting human beings, too.

TAKE A TRIP BY BOOK

When a particular object rouses your interest, go to the public library and learn as much as possible about it. Find out about the species of tree whose beauty caught your attention. Go back into old newspaper files to discover the history of the old house that wakened your curiosity.

If a foreign country rouses your interest, explore it by way of the printed page. Read everything you can about it. This sort of interest pays big dividends.

Young William Hickling Prescott, 1796-1859. was struck in the left eye by a crust of bread while he was attending Harvard. He lost the sight of the eye, and shortly after graduation his right eye also began to fail him. He was forced to abandon his career as a lawyer and spend most of his time in a darkened room. Being so nearly blind, he had to depend on readers for information about the outside world.

All the same he developed into a famous traveler, not only in space but in time. He became a noted historian; the work that flowed from his pen was prodigious. He could not reread or revise his first drafts, yet he is classed among America's finest writers. And the pages of his **History of the Conquest of Mexico** and **History of the Conquest of Peru** glow with the vivid colors of countries he had never seen but had none the less observed with great care.

A KNOWLEDGE OF ORCHIDS WINS A TRIP

John Gary, a young botany major at the University of Southern California, had a burning desire to see Hawaii but no money to finance the trip. Instead, he began to read every book he could find on the subject.

One night at a friend's house he met two men who were from Hawaii. Young Gary entered into a conversation with them about their homeland. He displayed so much detailed information that they were convinced he had lived on the islands.

Finally one of the men said his hobby was growing orchids.

John Gary replied, "Then you must have among your collection the only native orchid Hawaii can boast of."

The man emphatically denied that there was such a flower, but John Gary stuck to his guns.

"It doesn't cut much of a figure as an orchid," he said. "All the same, the only place it grows is on Mount Haleakala on Maui."

The orchid fancier continued to shake his head. But the other man, who was a botanist associated with the University of Hawaii, looked at the young man in astonishment.

"Yes," he agreed, "you're right. But few people have ever heard of it."

The botanist was so impressed by Gary's knowledge of Hawaiian plant life that he offered him a trip to Hawaii, all expenses paid, to serve as his field assistant the following summer.

DIVIDENDS FROM YOUR TREASURES

You may not be a Prescott or a John Gary, but we will guarantee that every treasure you drop into your knapsack will pay you dividends. Drama coaches have seen this happen to their students after just a few weeks of observation practice.

"When my students first come to me," said David Alexander, one of Jack Lemmon's former coaches and teacher to many stars, "most of them are leading small, inhibited lives. But as they begin to discover the joy that comes with observing everything around them, they become more vital and responsive. You wouldn't recognize them as the same people who first entered my class."

Change will take place in you as you begin to climb out of your rut. Soon life will hold more zest for you. And many of the things that you had taken for granted will be transformed into strange and wonderful objects.

Presently you will grow aware that your horizons are broadening in other ways. You will find your conversation enriched by the new knowledge. Your fresh interest will increase your circle of acquaintasnces and make new friends for you, people with similar tastes.

Then one day this store of observation you've collected will provide you with a magic combination to enable you to fulfill your brightest dream-to achieve a new position, to make a fascinating trip, to amass a fortune, or just to enjoy life instead of merely living it.

Here are exercises to help you. They have been gathered from those who felt that the instinct of observation was valuable enough to devise means for sharpening it, not only for use on the stage of the theater, but on the stage of life as well.

Exercise 1 **An exercise given by the late Constantin Stanislavski to his pupils**

This exercise can be transformed into and absorbing parlor game. Have a moderator assign some object in the room to every member of the group. Each person examines his own object for thirty seconds, after which the lights go out.

Then each in turn describes what he has seen. You will be amazed at the discrepancies between actuality and your mental picture of it. But with time and practice your perception will become more accurate.

A variation of this exercise may be found in Rudyard Kipling's **Kim.** Young Kim is presented with a tray of various objects and asked to enumerate and describe them after a few seconds of observation. As the individual becomes proficient, more objects may be added.

Another form of this exercise is to look at a picture for a minute and then put down in writing all you have seen. At first you will probably find many gaps in your memory. But with practice you will begin to recognize more and more details.

Exercise 2 **An exercise used by the FBI to train their men in observation**

When you enter a strange room-this can be done in many public buildings without attracting attention-give yourself a few minutes and then come out of the room and try to draw up its plan, locating furniture, rugs, pictures, ash trays, books, and the position and appearance of any people present. Do not omit colors.

You will be amazed at the discrepancy between your mental plan and the real one. But with practice you will find yourself able presently to take in most details at a glance. FBI men practice this exercise constantly, using homes, public halls or any other unfamiliar building in which they may find themselves.

Exercise 3 **Exercise used by the authors**

Assign yourself a small area which lies along your way to work. Observe everything possible while passing by. Do not pause to make a careful research. Later, jot down what you have noticed. The next day check your details against reality and try to add fresh details-but also without lingering.

You will scarcely believe the number of objects you missed the first time. Keep up this little game, every day for a week. As your sense of observation becomes more proficient choose a fresh area and increase the radius of your attention.

Or instead of choosing an area, you can arbitrarily select a certain period in the day to be especially observant. If you must attend a social function which frightens you, plan to do your exercise during this time. **Make** an uncritical but observant appraisal of your fellow guests with an eye to remembering everything about them.

Besides developing your powers of observation this outward-going exercise will help you overcome any sense of self-consciousness.

three

Attention

ATTENTION : MAGIC KEY NUMBER TWO

YOU are now ready to turn second magic key in its lock and thus to open up for yourself even greater possibilities in the performance of your life's role. This is the magic key of **attention.** Actually observation and attention are correlates.

Observation is a passive function. When you practice it you are like the spectator at a sports event or in a theater. You see what is going on and you can enjoy it immensely. But the thrill of participating in the game is denied you.

When you practice attention you are taking the second important step to joining the actors on the stage of life instead of remaining among the faceless spectators watching from the pit below.

OBSERVATION MAIMED BY INATTENTION

In fact, you will discover that unless you train yourself to be attentive you will not be able to rely on your powers of observation. Look back on your experiences with the observation exercise and you will become aware of a curious phenomenon. Sometimes you were able to remember distinctly almost every detail of a room. Other times you discovered that the room turned out to be a blur in recollection, or that you inserted furniture that was not there and color combinations that came straight from your imagination.

You may find, too, that your memory at times is vague about the physical appearance of certain individuals. You are unable to picture them clearly. Sometimes even the sequence of events or the gist of conversations escapes you.

Such vagueness isn't unusual, though it may be disconcerting. It happens to everybody and is epitomized by the symbol of the absent-minded professor. There is no such thing as true absent-mindedness in a normal person. Your mind is never an empty blank. It is only inattentive to the subject at hand because it is concentrating on something else.

AN ACTOR AND HIS ATTENTION

An actor cannot afford to be inattentive on stage. He would miss his cues, forget his lines and confuse his fellow players.

A good actor realizes that there's more to attention than just being on the alert to keep the mechanical routine of the play in smooth running order. An actor often must repeat the same performance over and over, matinees and evenings for six months to a year, or even several years.

Think of it! Reciting the same lines, listening to the same lines going through the same business over and over. It could result in an enervating tedium that would quickly transform the actor into a polished automation.

How then does the good actor manage seem as natural, fresh and spontaneous during his hundredth time performance as on opening night? He does it by following one simple basic rule.

THE ACTOR: ALWAYS ATTENTIVE TO HIS FELLOW PLAYER

True, an actor knows what that player is going to say. He has heard it all many times before. And the actor knows what he is going to answer. These words were written for him by the playwright. Instead of being their originator, he will be their interpreter.

How then does he manage? Simply by blotting out of his mind all past performances and coming to this one though it were fresh and new. He knows the lines, so they will come to him automatically, and he will not need to concentrate on them. Instead, he concentrates not on **what** is being spoken but **how** it is being spoken, as though he were hearing it for the first time.

By being attentive he realizes that, appearances to the contrary, nothing is being repeated, after all. He may, for example, hear a different inflection in the other player's voice that calls for a subtle change in his own response. It is like a game of tennis between two pros.

In this way, a show like **My Fair Lady** remained vital and fresh to audiences even at the close of the engagement. Two pros, Rex Harrison and Julie Andrews, weren't content with rendering mechanical perfection to their lines during their long contact with the play. They never once made the mistake, characteristic of beginners-of performing for the **audience.**

Instead, they involved themselves in each other and their fellow players as though no spectators were present. Thus they responded freshly to new stimuli created by that day's different moods.

Now, how about the little scenes you must play throughout your day? You have an advantage over the stage actor. Your words are your own. You can manipulate the plot at will and change the action. Do you bring a fresh approach to these scenes or do you go through them routinely without bothering about the moods or reactions of your fellow players?

YOU AND DAVID NIVEN

If you're going through the scenes routinely, you're not alone in making this mistake. David Niven told us the following story about himself. Back in 1935, at the start of his career, he played his first role for the screen. It was only a small part in an MGM movie called **A Feather in Her Hat,** starring Billie Burke.

Niven, along with several distinguished guests, had been invited to the first private showing of the film at the home of the late Irving Thalberg and his wife, Norma Shearer. David held his breath in apprehension at first. But when he saw himself he let it out slowly.

"Not bad," he thought. "Not bad at all."

He was pleased, when the lights came on again, to find his opinion echoed by most of the important people in the room. Miss Shearer, Connie Bennett, humorist Robert Benchley and Louis B. Mayer all were unqualified in their praise.

Niven's triumph should have been complete, but it wasn't because throughout all these compliments one man sat silent. To Niven he was the most important one present because he was the world renowned master of comedy Charlie Chaplin.

Finally Niven found enough courage to ask him pointblank for his opinion.

Chaplin replied gravely, "You don't listen well, Mr. Niven. And you will never be a really good actor until you learn to do so."

Niven took the advice to heart. One of the qualities that make him a fine actor today is that quality of listening with interest and expectation to everything being said, as though he were hearing it for the first time.

WHY NOT FOLLOW CHARLIE CHAPLIN'S ADVICE?

Have you, like Niven, been putting on what you believed was a fine performance and seen it somehow fall flat?

The idea you wanted to sell that didn't go over?

The promotion you expected that didn't come through?

The marriage that started out so romantically that has somehow turned cold and empty?

The fault may lie in not listening to the other fellow, not to what he is saying but to **how** he is saying it, and listening with warmth and interest.

Maybe that idea was a fine one, but because you weren't attentive to the mood of the man to whom you presented it and left him out of the picture, you couldn't get to first base.

Maybe you didn't get that promotion your work should have earned you because you didn't give the impression of being interested in others. A computer can be efficient, too, but it can't simulate the quality of warm personal attentiveness that is so necessary to the successful conduct of any business.

May be your marriage has resulted in a sense of boredom and estrangement because you are sure you know everything your mate has to say and have stopped listening or taking a interest in the other's viewpoint.

INATTENTION CAN SPELL DISASTER

Not only does inattention narrow our involvement in life, it also can pave the way for disaster. History is full of the stories of great civilizations that have failed, not from strong forces outside themselves but from the decay that follows inattention.

If Louis XVI and Marie Antoinette had listened more carefully to what their hungry people were saying there might have been no French Revolution and they would have saved their own necks. If the Russian Czars had been more attentive to their people's needs, there might have been no Bolshevist revolution.

Look back into the history of your community and review the bad events that have spoiled the image of your city. Very likely you'll find that they were due to apathy. How many of us are interested in the plight of slum dwellers? In the inequalities that spring from bias of one kind or another? In the welfare of children other than our own?

How many times, for instance, after a painful scandal hits the newspapers, have you and your neighbors been justified in saying. "If only we'd given the young people of our community more attention, this tragedy need never have happened."

INATTENTION AND ITS PENALTY

Look back now into your personal, history. Surely, you remember occasions when inattention inflicted humiliation and inconvenience far out of proportion to the amount of attention which would have averted the crisis?

How many employers, for instance, have been left in the lurch by valuable employees whom they have been treating like obedient robots? And how many hostesses planning an important dinner party have been faced with the loss of a cook because they haven't troubled to establish the bond of loyalty that springs from personal contact?

How many times have we lost out because we've shown lack of interest in someone, only to learn later that this individual could have furthered our careers or helped us achieve some cherished project?

There's saying in the film industry, "Don't neglect the office boy. One day he may be head of the studio."

THREE OBSTACLES TO ATTENTION

We list three main causes for inattention. Perhaps you will be able to think of more.

1. Boredom
2. Prejudice
3. Egotism

BOREDOM

When someone bores us, we tend to blank out while he's talking and busy ourselves with own thoughts. We think this action is undetected, but it shows on our faces. The next time you find yourself with an uninteresting person, try the following trick to help you play your role more satisfactorily.

Repeat to yourself the words of the old Mexican proverb, "Every head a world." Then make up your mind to bring all your attention to this individual's world with the purpose of exploring it effectively.

You may not like the territory you find there, but you can increase your knowledge of human nature and also practice the fine art of tolerance. And perhaps the fellow you always considered boring turns out to be an interesting chap after all. Perhaps he is handicapped by inadequate powers of expression and only needs kind attention to spill out his inner world of treasures.

PREJUDICE

Prejudice, the second of the obstacles we've listed, doesn't spring from passive boredom but from active resistance. It's hard to listen to people who are making statements we don't agree with.

Why not try something else? Instead of closing your ears the next time someone espouses an idea or a cause you don't approve of, listen without reservations to what he has to say. Your calm attentiveness may make him aware of the flaws in his arguments. Or perhaps, you may even discover reason is on his side. At the very least, it will broaden your own outlook on life by taking time to explore the unique world of another.

EGOTISM

Egotism makes people deaf to the needs of the other fellow. Being absorbed in themselves they haven't time to show constructive interest in anyone else. They're like the actor who sacrifices the play and the fellow members of his troupe to hog the spotlight for himself. In short, a ham!

You've seen the fellow who rushes up to guest after guest at gatherings with a hearty handshake and a cheery, "Oh, hello there! I'm so glad to see you! You look wonderful!"

Flattering, except that while he's speaking he hardly glances at you. His eyes are too busy roaming around the room for another victim.

You have met the person so in love with his own voice that he never stops chattering. Perhaps you've heard the criticism, "She's attractive, but I can't take too much of her-she never shuts her mouth," or "He's an interesting man, but he wears you out bending your ear."

Perhaps you have a tendency to be an egotist. Check yourself at the next party. Do you give whole and earnest attention to the person you're greeting as though he were the only one in the room? Or do you jump from one person to another without stopping to make anything really personal? When you're in a conversation, do you listen as wholeheartedly as you talk?

If not, put a rein on your tongue and stretch you ears. Because:

ATTENTION PAYS HIGH DIVIDENDS

Here's how one man turns his genuine interest in others into financial success. He's Stanley Shapiro, the famous movie writer who collaborated on **Pillow Talk, Operation Petticoat** and other film hits.

At any Hollywood party where he is a guest you will find Mr. Shapiro one of the most attentive persons in the room. He is also one of the most popular. His genuine interest in people has them talking freely about themselves. So he doesn't just spin his stories out of his own head. The characters he writes about are real. They are revealed to him because of his absorbing interest in actual people.

You needn't be a writer to make listening pay off. The interest you show in them enlivens your own personality, makes you more attractive and likable and may even open the necessary door to enable you to realize a cherished dream.

By this method the late Mrs. Eleanor Roosevelt accomplished much in her lifetime. She was known as the First Lady of the World, not because she was the wife of a great President or because she was the spokesman of any powerful group. Her success in getting the wholehearted cooperation necessary to carry out her manifold projects originated in her genuine interest in people. It shone through every word and act and made those with whom she came in contact eager to be of service to her.

We personally observed how she was always so warmly intent on co-operating in an interview that the story about her invariably went her way. Many celebrities fail to realize this vital art in presenting a better image to reporters. But Mrs. Roosevelt wasn't just attentive to reporters or those who might do something for her. Here is an example of how deep was her concern for others.

Every year she sent a modest birthday remembrance to one of her god-children, the daughter of a former gardener. She never forgot, even after the girl had grown up, married and had a family of her own.

The last birthday gift came from Mrs. Roosevelt while on her deathbed. Even in her suffering she was able to give her attention to making someone else happy.

To help the reader develop the valuable art of attention we provide some interesting exercises.

EXERCISE 1 **An exercise given by Estelle Harman who conducts a highly successful Hollywood drama school and has had as students Diane Baker, Tony Curtis and Rock Hudson. She calls it** "The Awareness Exercise".

This exercise requires two people and can be adapted to make a hilarious parlor game.

Two people sit facing each other and begin a conversation. There is only one rule—neither one may say anything about himself but must always direct his remarks to and about the other person.

Here is a sample.

She: "I like your tie." (Said, perhaps in a voice implying dislike for it.) .

The reply cannot then be concerned with the tie but must relate to the speaker. If the second person has been alert enough to catch the tone of voice, he will reply, "No, you don't really like my tie. You are just saying so to be facetious."

When the first person picks up the conversation he must again direct his remarks to and about the person in front of him. He might say something like. "Why you so sensitive?"

And so on.

According to Miss Harman, in a fast exchange of this kind with the emphasis on "What do I think of him?" instead of "What does he think of me?" people lose their self-consciousness.

"I've noticed that within an hour or two my pupils show a new alertness toward one another and don't remain isolated in their little corners, "she told us. Miss Harman suggests a solo variation of this exercise which may be practiced by commuters on their way to work. Pick out one of your fellow travelers and take a good look at him. Puzzle over him, asking questions of yourself about him. What is the reason for the quizzical expression on his face? Why does he sit with his shoulders drooped? What a strange way of holding his hands! What is he thinking of?

You may never know for certain, but you will enjoy a new expansion in your horizons.

EXERCISE 2 **An exercise given by Jeff Corey, director, actor and well-known drama coach, to sharpen attentiveness in observation**

Practice the exercises at the end of Chapter 2 on "Observation," but with this difference. Upon entering a room you intend to "observe," arbitrarily tab it as the room in which some famous personage, whom you admire, lived and died.

Say to yourself that the room is exactly as he left it, the opportunity to understand the secrets of a great personality. Then look about. Note how each article jumps out at you either by its aptness or its incongruity with the facts of the departed person as revealed in his biography or history. Later you may be surprised at how easily you can describe the room.

This same technique may be applied to people. Say to yourself, during introduction, for instance, "What a privilege to be meeting the Queen of England. Now I shall be able to find out her likes and dislikes." With this attitude your attention becomes immeasurably sharpened. And who knows, you may even find your new acquaintance every bit as interesting as a queen.

Dr. Wendell Johnson, authority on semantics and author of the standard work **People in Quandaries**, gives a variation of this exercise as follows:

Stand on the corner of any busy street and pretend you are in a foreign city whose language is unknown to you Because you are in a strange country and have to get along in it, you must make yourself conversant with these people—their customs, their dress and most especially their personalities. Since you cannot understand the language you must concentrate on their gestures and the expressions of their faces to divine what they are thinking and saying.

This technique can also be applied to a party or any other public gathering which you dread attending. Pretend you are a member of an expedition covering a strange ritual in a far-off country. Tell yourself that every detail is necessary for an exact appraisal of this ceremony.

Forget that you may be acquainted with some of the guests; look at them with the eyes of an observant scientist. You will find yourself learning new things about your own civilization and at the same time losing the self-consciousness which comes with centering on yourself.

EXERCISE 3 **An exercise to bring back romance into the lives of married couples, contributed by Lajos Egri, noted playwright, author of** *The Art of Dramatic Writing* **and private instructor to many famous stage and screen writers.**

Tell yourself that your mate is an exciting stranger whom you are meeting for the first time and want to get to know better. You will then begin to see him or her afresh. Things you had not noticed in your mate before, or had forgotten, will come to light.

If you play this second-courtship game faithfully over a period of time you will find your mate beginning to shine in just those qualities which you are recognizing now and which have been buried so long, simply from lack of attention or appreciation..

And you will very likely begin to fall in love all over again.

four

Your Physical Apparatus

PRESENCE: MAGIC KEY NUMBER THREE

IF YOU have been practicing your observation exercises, especially those involving people, you will have become aware of the part "presence" plays in helping a person put on a good performance. Presence, a difficult word to define, is that which makes some people convincing by lending them an authoritative or attractive air. In short, presence makes a man stand out among his fellows. Few realize that it springs from complete control of the body, whether arrived at intuitively or through conscious effort.

AN ACTOR AND HIS PRESENCE

A good actor knows he can't be content just being what he is. He supplements his natural equipment with conscious training, for he, above all others, realizes the value of his body in expressing himself. It is to him what a violin or piano is to a musician, or brush, paints and easel are to an artist.

Sometimes, of course, the previous careers of actors have prepared them for the difficult roles they must portray. But Lancaster was formerly a trapeze artist and William Holden a stunt man. These man like to do thseir own stunts far the screen.

But many actors must go through periods of arduous training to help them perform certain roles realistically. For his part in **The Champion Kirk** Douglas spent long hours with Mushy Callahan, the noted fight trainer. He went through the rigorous exercises followed by professional fighters to prepare themselves, jumping rope a couple of hours a day and running long distances.

He sparred with a succession of partners whom Callahan provided, getting "a fist full of face every time I zigged when I should have zagged," as Kirk puts it. All this pummeling and bruising, all the strenuous exercise to which he exposed himself was for the sole purpose of enabling him to give a realistic performance in one screen role.

Debbie Reynolds spent hours rehearsing her dance routines for **The Unsinkable Molly Brown.** One of the most difficult dances had to be performed in long woollen underwear, an oversized sequined dress, boots, a leather belt and with a heavy gun. The dance routines in the picture were all so arduous that Debbie's weight had fallen from one hundred and six pounds to ninety-six by the time the picture was completed. However, without such wholehearted subjection of her body to the demands of the role, she would never have succeeded in giving the delightful portrayal of Molly which caught the imagination of the world.

WHAT ABOUT YOUR PRESENCE?

You don't need to go through such grueling exercises to play your role in life properly, but it will pay you well to give attention to the image the world sees. Look at yourself in the mirror as though you were a stranger. Bring the art of observation you've cultivated to bear on yourself. What do you see?

Do your clothes droop as though they were ashamed to be seen on you? Do you have a built-in slouch? Are your shoulders stooped, is your chest concave? Have your clothes become so tight-fitting that you're squeezed in them like a sausage?

If so, ponder this. Before you utter a word, your presence speaks for you in whatever venture you may undertake. A trim, neat buoyant look increase your self-assurance, as well as making you generally more attractive to others.

AN ACTOR'S BUGABOO

Excess weight can cause us all trouble in failing to present a good self image. It adds years to our appearance and it tends to make us move awkwardly instead of with the grace and precision nature intended for us.

In this day of the wide screen, where even a few added pounds show up plainly, motion picture and TV actors and actresses have to avoid overweight at all costs. Many of them patronize gymnasiums to shed those extra pounds or keep them off. Any day of the week you will find the stars at Terry Hunt's famous gymnasium in Beverly Hills. There they exercise under supervision to keep their bodies in shape.

William Gargan, some years before he won his courageous battle against throat cancer, went to Hunt to lose forty pounds so he could make a comeback. Jose Ferrer lost twenty pounds there before he started a TV series.

Laurence Harvey doesn't wait for the pounds to show up. Whenever he is in town he is a frequent visitor at Hunt's gym. He even had a rock steam bath and gymnasium built at the home he leased in Beverly Hills.

THERE'S MORE AT STAKE THAN WEIGHT

Exercise does more than keep you trim. It also keeps the body young as well as flexible. Maurice Chevalier in his seventies and Fred Astaire in his sixties are still performing their arduous dance routines. Men like Cary Grant, Bob Cummings and Rex Harrison, who are all in their fifties and sixties, continue playing romantic leads.

How do they manage to keep the number of years they've lived from changing the kind of roles they play? If we know that secret we can keep ourselves active participants in the drama of life instead of consigning ourselves to the sidelines of age.

THE SECRET OF KEEPING A YOUTHFUL BODY AND MIND

Why do some people age rapidly while others still remain active? We discussed this problem with Dr. Laurence E. Morehouse, Professor of Physical Education at the University of California at Los Angeles and author of **Sports Medicine for Trainers** and other valuable textbooks.

Dr. Morehouse, who helped set up the training program for American astronauts, states flatly that unless there is some pathological disorder such as arthritis, men and women should never give up physical activity. It is inactivity, not age, that weakens the system. It causes muscles to grow flabby, and the vascular system to become so weakened that the body can no longer function normally.

BUT OH, THOSE EXERCISES!

So we must exercise to stay fit.

But when someone says "Exercise" we immediately think of those long, tedious hours of gymnastics we were put through at school. We shy away from the very thought of them.

If you are one of those who hate the thought of exercise, here are some interesting but little-known facts that may help you to change your attitude. These came to light during experiments conducted by Dr. Morehouse and his associates. The experiments proved that as little as six minutes a week of exercise causes a noticeable improvement in resistance to fatigue, increases ability to do prolonged intellectual work, and simulates interest in more strenuous physical activities such as dancing bowling and swimming.

Why? By interviewing his subjects Dr. Morehouse discovered that this brief weekly emphasis on exercise had brought about a surprising change of consciousness in them. It was as though some force deep within had been alerted to the fact that "care is being taken" and had instigated a complete overhaul of their daily habits in the interest of health.

WHAT A BONUS!.

Isn't an exhilarated and more expansive life worth as little as six minutes a week of exercise? So if you haven't the time or the inclination for a crash program, remember that your body is grateful and will respond in many fruitful ways even to any attention you may give it.

Here are a few rules from both Terry Hunt and Dr. Morehouse that will insure your getting maximum benefit from your exercises.

1 Choose whatever exercises you decide to perform with an eye to giving as many of your muscles a workout as possible.

2 Read your instructions carefully. An exercise performed the wrong way can do more harm than good.

3 Keep your mind concentrated on the part of your body that you are working on. Concentration insures your doing exercise with special emphasis on the muscles that need to be benefited. Some authorities even claim concentration also acts in draw blood to that area. And blood both heals and creates muscle tone, eliminating flabbiness.

4 Don't overdo your exercising on the first goround. Many of us have the feeling that if a little exercise helps, a great deal will be infinitely better. And so we may overdo, strain ourselves, get discouraged and stop exercising altogether. It's better,

therefore, to exercise by the clock. This eliminates all tendency to rush.

5 Don't exercise vigorously when you've been out late the night before, and especially if you've been doing a lot of drinking. It won't help a hangover and it might do your muscles harm.

6 Don't forget to exercise when you are losing weight. Otherwise you'll be flabby. One of the best ways to take additional weight off your midsection is by stretching.

7. When you do sit-ups, place your hands on your abdomen muscles to be sure you are using them and not the hip flexor muscles. The hip flexor muscles get enough exercise already in the simple act of sitting. It's your abdominal wall that grows weak from sedentary habits. This causes the pelvis to tilt out its load of heavy viscera and you have the pot belly. Sit-ups performed using the abdominal muscles will train the bowl of the pelvis to lie level, so that it can perform its function of holding the viscera in place, causing you to cut inches from your waistline.

STEALING SOME EXERCISES

Besides one's regular exercise period, Dr. Morehouse suggests using the many opportunities for exercising that present themselves during the course of the day. Here are a few suggestions.

Always walk down the stairs instead of using an elevator if you are below the fifth floor.

Whenever you have a short distance to go, practice the posture walk - at West Point they call it "Keeping your buttocks level." Dr. Morehouse, who terms it "tucking in your buttocks," explains that by tightening them and tucking them in as you walk, you level your pelvis, and this automatically gives you a slenderer waistline.

At the same time you are keeping your pelvis level keep your chest bone slightly up. A quarter of an inch is sufficient. To do this, imagine you have a wad of tin-foil or a marble in the hollow just above your breastbone which you want to keep from falling our. If you think of that marble and your level pelvis you can forget shoulders, arms and back. They will all fall automatically into place.

You can use the posture exercise while walking. Stand up and practice it whenever you answer your phone. .

TAKE A GOOD LONG LOOK AT YOUR HOUSECAT

You can learn something from the cat. It spends much of its time sleeping yet is lithe, agile sod strong when the occasion requires. About the only exercise the cat takes is an occasional stretch, during which it tenses its whole body so that the muscles pull against each other. Pitting one muscle against another to form a resistance is what is known as an isotonic exercise.

With this secret in mind practice converting your irritations into body-building exercise. It can be done. Vivacious Laura Huxley, wife of the late Aldous Huxley, psychological counselor and writer of the best seller **You Are Not the Target**, handles her passing irritations in this constructive way.

"Noise used to get me very upset," she told the authors. "Then I discovered that my feeling of irritation was full of energy that could be directed into these muscular flexions which are isotonic exercises. They are marvelous body toners. What I do is to tense and relax my thighs in rhythm to the noise. It required conscious effort at first but now it has become so habitual that I do it automatically. And it has paid off because in the process I've lost an inch or two around my thighs".

Mrs. Huxley has discovered that she has not only trimmed her figure with the surplus energy created by her irritations, but has also robbed those irritations of their power to cloud her reasoning ability.

Try it yourself. After a few weeks of isotonic tone-up see what happens in that department and bring a tape measure to your waistline, too. What you discover will encourage you to continue the experiment.

SO WHAT ABOUT GLAMOR?

Exercise may tone the body, but of itself it doesn't insure grace or poise. And since grace is an essential element of actresses in particular, most young starlets are sent to charm schools as part of their training.

However, we will content ourselves here with only a few tips from Zina Provendie, well-know Hollywood drama coach. While she was in New York, Miss Provendie prepared a course for the famous Grace Downs Model and Air Career School.

"One of the principal things wrong with women today," explains Miss Provendie, "is that we're afraid to be ourselves. However, we must take care that we do not interpret 'being ourselves' as giving us the right to indulge in ugly, awkward poses because they seem 'natural' to us. A woman should adopt and make her own those postures that give the impression of greater femininity if she wishes to show herself off to the best advantage." .

Here are some of Miss Provendie's rules for accomplishing this.

A man may sit as he pleases just so he's relaxed about it. On the other hand a woman who sprawls, far from appearing relaxed and graceful, looks gauche.

When a woman sits she shouldn't aim at the chair with her behind. She should back up to it, feel for it with the calf of her right or left leg, and then lower herself with the leg acting as a lever. When she reaches the seat she should slide into place and relax against the back. She should never sit on the edge of her chair as though she expected to fly away at any moment.

If a woman crosses her legs, the leg that does the crossing should be well over the other so that the calf of one does not rest on the calf of the other, for this distorts the leg. Also, for the same reason, don't tuck your feet well back under your chair.

When you walk put one foot in front of the other and don't straddle or point your toes out. Pointing your toes out, incidentally, is bad on the posture, for it distorts the alignment of your skeleton.

If a man offers to light a woman's cigarette she may incline slightly toward him, but let him come most of the way. She should hold her cigarette loosely, not grasp it like a fiend, and draw on it lightly, her hand slightly curled. She should never hold her cigarette in the corner of her mouth or speak while it is between her lips. She should not smoke it to the bitter end.

Stanislavski used to say that if the eyes were the mirror of the soul, the fingertips might be regarded as the expression of the body. Then let your hands express yourself naturally. Women who are still in the Victorian era can be recongnized by the way they clasp their hands. Even today, figures of the classic opera still sing with their hands clasped in the same way. But if you leave your hands alone they'll drop naturally and the fingers will curl slightly.

THE MIRROR OF THE SOUL

As for the eyes, they really are the expression of the soul. So instead of jumping into the breach with words, let your eyes do the talking whenever possible. At least, let them accentuate your words.

Try this experiment. Look into the mirror and say with feeling. "I hate you." If you are truly feeling it you will see that ugly sentiment plainly mirrored in your eyes. Then try "I love you," with fervent feeling.

Now cover your mouth with your hand. Think, "I love you," You still see it in your eyes. But shade your eyes with your hand so that you can see only your mouth in the mirror and say, "I love you," forming your words silently. The mouth hardly changes in normal speech and you seek nothing at all.

NOW FOR YOU MEN

There are certain symbols that characterize masculinity. Actors make use of these symbols or their reverse to bring a sense of realism to their parts. For instance, to smoke a cigarette with the lighted end protruding between the fingers outward is normal and masculine. Peter O'Toole, who played the title role in **Lawrence of Arabia** and King Henry in **Becket** normally smokes his cigarette in this fashion. But when he wishes to portray a weak character he turns the lighted end inward. This gives him an air of foppishness.

Similarly, casual rather than fastidious dress is associated with masculinity. When the sophisticated George Hamilton was signed to work with Richard Boone in A **Thunder of Drums**, Zina Provendie warned him, "You're playing with a man who knows all the angles of masculinity. If you want to hold your own with him, get rid of your cuff links and your stiff collar. Come on the set as casually dressed as possible."

Boone achieved his appearance of great masculinity in his role of Paladin by using Dr. Morehouse's exercise of "tucking in the buttocks." This not only tightens the muscles of the buttocks but also lends a masculine assertiveness to the posture of legs and torso. Even the voice takes on a stronger, more forceful intonation.

Another trick you may find useful is to imagine yourself planted firmly over the magnetic center of the earth. Now consciously draw up the earth force from this center through your feet into your legs and from there into your whole body until you are suffused with it. Do this without tension and you will find yourself not only standing straighter but also feeling a great sense of vitality and power.

Alexander Mackendrick, the English director of **The Sweet Smell of Success,** found this trick useful in a critical situation. He had been engaged to direct **The Devil's Disciple,** but wanted to be released.

When he asked Burt Lancaster to let him out, Lancaster lost his temper. In his anger he charged over some furniture toward Mackendrick with the idea of punching him. Fortunately he was some distance away and Mackendrick, who didn't want to fight, had time to prepare for the onslaught.

He remembered the trick of drawing power from the earth and jumped to his feet, Planted them firmly on the ground and concentrated on filling his body with power. Lancaster was stopped short by Mackendrick's formidable appearance. He gave in, quietly paid the director and released him from the picture without another argument.

PARALYSIS BY ANALYSIS

You may wish to augment these suggestions for better appearance with others, which you can easily find by consulting the many fine books of this nature on the market. But here's a word of caution. Once you've learned the rules-forget about them. Otherwise, you will find yourself hamstrung by the very routines you had expected to help you.

In athletics this condition is known as Paralysis by Analysis. This athlete who is "paralyzed by analysis" is the one who is putting so much attention on his movements that he is unable to concentrate on the game itself. The beginning golfer, for instance, must first learn the position of his feet and hands and the stances required to make the various swings with his club. But after he has mastered all these techniques he is warned to take his attention away from them and focus on the placement of the ball.

Stanislavski applied this rule of forgetting the rules to the field of acting by instructing his students to concentrate on their objective, letting the necessary action flow out naturally. Such naturalness is the secret of a small child's charm: His movements are not premeditated but spring spontaneously from his desires. Today those of us actors on the stage of life who wish to approximate this same easy mobility of action must learn the lesson all over again.

We must get on more intimate terms with the body that we have been using, abusing and ignoring for so many years.

REALLY GETTING ACQUAINTED WITH YOUR BODY

Dr. Morehouse suggests shedding your clothes now and braving a full-length mirror, standing in the nude in order to make a frank examination of yourself.

"We have a puritan idea about this. We think it's narcissistic," he explained. "But it's the best way I know of to come to terms with your physical self. Even though you are sure you look pretty awful, try to think of yourself as being more beautiful or handsome that what you see.

"Next, practice rhythmic movements to get the feel of your body in motion. Be as free as possible in these movements.

"Give a few minutes every day to this self appraisal and rhythmic movement exercise. This interest in yourself will initiate the same kind of feedback phenomenon the six-minute weekly exercise period did for my subjects. It flashes back to that deep center of Self the message, 'Someone is interested. Someone is noticing.'"

RELY ON THE CENTER

Once that center of the self is activated, you can confidently leave the management of your body to its care. The late Michael Chekhov, the great drama coach and director and Stanislavski's most famous student, had an exercise that should help you visualize and strengthen your sense of the center.

Imagine this center as being located in your chest and possessing unlimited vitality. Allow it to fill your body with that vitality. You can picture it as flowing in tides of warm, radiant light through all your muscles and down the channels of your bones. Consciously feel the vibrations of that glowing energy and mentally go through your body, opening every tight muscle to its light.

Imagine that every movement you make emanates from that center. When you are walking, send the center from your chest to travel before you. Let yourself be guided by that imaginary wheel of light. Give your emotions over to it and let go of your own conscious controls. You will be surprised at how easy and smooth all your movements become.

THE REWARDS

After only a few weeks of practice you'll find yourself meeting adventures and problems of life with a greater zest than ever before. This new self-assurance is the results of your becoming part of your body again.

Many of us have so divorced ourselves from our bodies that we have lost a dimensions of our lives. As we reunite ourselves with this dimension we make it available as a tool to help us express more richly our individualities.

This acquiring of presence transforms an otherwise competent but uninspired actor into a magnetic star. It will do the same for you. Try it and see.

five

Tension

THE TENSION BUGABOO

WE MAY train our physical bodies to perform very well in the give and take of daily life. But no matter how free we may feel under ordinary circumstances, there come opportunities which we are in danger of muffing dismally, and for one reason-**tension.**

Tensions are the curse of civilized life. They cause us to say the wrong things. They betray us into behaving timorously or aggressively, or they keep us from acting at all. They tie us in knots precisely when a cool and masterful approach is essential.

None of us is immune to these trying experiences, from the President in the White House to the timid student in the speech class. Executives of multimillion-dollar business get butterflies in their stomachs when they find it necessary to convince board members of the efficacy of some costly innovation. Wizard salesmen freeze up when they face prospect whose business is too important to lose.

No doubt you can recall the moments when nervous tension prevented you from playing your role convincingly and perhaps even caused you to appear ridiculous.

Mindful of such experiences you may envy the actor. He seems to have full control of himself before an audience with the power to annihilate his career. He goes through his lines with an air of confidence, even aplomb. Surely, we tell ourselves, he is a kind of superhuman who does not know the agony of tension.

DON'T BELIEVE IT!

Young actors just beginning their careers also have the impression that experienced actors are completely confident. They anticipate the time when, as seasoned performers, everything will be simple and easy for them. They are usually disillusioned by long-time professionals, who know the answers.

Rock Hudson gave a graphic illustration of the actor's dilemma when he was giving a lecture to a drama class conducted by his former coach, Estelle Harman. He was scheduled to talk for ten minutes, but he was still going strong two hours later and seemed to be thoroughly enjoying himself.

Finally one of the students, impressed by Rock's self-assurance, asked hopefully, "Mr. Hudson, when does an actor stop being tense and nervous?"

Rock, who was in his shirt sleeves, laughed and lifted his arms. His shirt was literally soaked with perspiration.

Gilan Golan, the young Israeli actress, received a similar reply from Vivien Leigh, star of such outstanding pictures as **Gone With the Wind** and **A Streetcar Named Desire.** Gila was about to make her acting debute in Stanley Kramer's **Ship of Fools,** and she was shaking with apprehension.

She turned to the apparently poised Miss Leigh, who was also in the film, and said, "How fortunate you are. I'm so nervous."

"Don't worry about that, Gila," Miss Leigh replied. "We are **all** nervous. And any time you see an actress who isn't tense before a performance, you know she's not much good."

DON'T BE ASHAMED OF NERVOUSNESS

Your nervous tensions come from sensitivity, and sensitivity is a valuable asset-it makes you more aware of life. The problem is to keep your tensions under control.

The professional actor **has** to learn this lesson in order to continue his career, for everything about his profession builds up tension. He must expose himself to countless thousands, among whom, he knows, are acid-penned critics ready to pick flaws in his performance. He must take the chance of failing in the brutal glare of the spotlight.

His power of speech is endangered if he allows tensions to take possession of him. They can cause such constricting let cramps that it becomes difficult for him to take a step.

Directors with multimillion dollar films on their hands are also afflicted by these body-wracking tensions. One morning during the filming of the costly war epic, **King Rat,** Bryan Forbes, the British director of **Seance on a Wet Afternoon,** found himself unable to get out of bed. His tensions were so bad that they had tied his lower back in knots and left him immobile.

Director Blake Edwards, who has suffered similar problems, told us Forbes called him to ask the name of a good chiropractor. Blake suggested his own, Dr. Joe J. Miller. After the adjustment Forbes was able to get up and go to work. However, for about a week thereafter, Dr. Miller was on hand each day to keep Forbes from tensing up again.

Stars also make use of chiropractic methods to help keep their tensions under control. Dr. Miller has numbered among his patients Frank Sinatra, Robert Taylor, Joan Crawford, Peter Falk and Audie Murphy.

Metro-Goldwyn-Mayer Studios recognizes the problem by keeping another chiropractor, Dr. James. J. Mitchell, on the payroll, He's there to help relax studio personnel when the tensions become too great.

Even when there's no danger to an actor of being completely immobilized tension, it can cause him to garble his lines or forget them altogether.

The fear of being hamstrung during a performance is so potent that it often results in occupational anxiety dreams. The late Humphrey Bogart, tough man of the screen, confessed to us in a moment of candor shortly before his death that he was plagued by just such a recurrent dream on the average of twice a month.

"In the dream I'm to open in a play." he told us. "I've neglected to study it. The curtain goes up and my cue is given. And I don't know a line. It's something you have to learn to live with."

STANISLAVSKI AND THE PIANO LEG

To demonstrate the difficulty of concentrating mentally while muscles are strained and taut, Stanislavski tried this experiment. He asked one of his students to lift the corner of piano so heavy that it required all his physical strength to comply.

While the student was holding up the piano, he was asked to perform simple mental exercises. First came an elementary problem in mathematics, then the recitation of well-known poetry, followed by the singing of a popular song. Finally, he was told to give an account of what he had done that morning before class.

The student found it impossible to perform the simple exercises while he was holding up the piano leg. As soon as he put it down he could easily run through them.

Stanislavski's experiment is a vivid example of what happens when we allow tensions to master us. We garble things. We make fools of ourselves. We fail in putting over an important project. We end the day with nausea or headache-or both.

In fact, we affect our health as well as business opportunities by allowing our nerves to take over at critical times. Medical experts tell us that many functional illnesses are directly caused by states of tension.

THE USE OF TENSION

Here is the paradox. Tension is useful. The complete elimination of tension, a state of absolute relaxation for which so many of us yearn, would also prohibit our getting a job done successfully.

This kind of relaxation, though beneficial in renewing the body during sleep, is of no use in meeting everyday problems. It will not untie any knots, win any races or achieve any worthwhile victories. The FBI does not want "calm" men on its force. Calm men would not have the alertness that comes with tension. They would be slow-thinking and slow-moving. Similarly, no calm athlete can win a race or a tennis match. The most magnetic actors are those who also possess a great deal of nervous tension. This is because nervous tension is filled with restrained energy that can be put to good use if properly channeled.

The following experiment was conducted by a team of psychologists which included Dr. Samuel Harman, psychology professor at Los Angeles City College, who described it to us. Photographs of a number of subjects were taken in one of three different poses. The first depicted a completely relaxed mood, the second a tensely active mood and the third the midway point between the two, which might be described as the mood of balanced tension.

These pictures were shown to a group of students, who were then asked to pick out the photographs of those whose personalities most appealed to them. Upon analyzing the results, the psychologists discovered that the majority of students had rejected the photographs of the models for the first and second mood as being too passive or neurotically tense. They had selected the subjects who depicted the mood of balanced tension as the ones who appeared to be best adjusted to life.

BALANCED TENSION

Granted then that the state of balanced tension is the ideal one, the basis of the best-liked personality and the lodestone to getting things done efficiently, the question is how to achieve it.

Actors and actresses, who must face the problem continually, have their own unique solutions.

Doris Day simply talks herself into relaxing.

"I find the very word 'relax' relaxing in itself," she told us. "So I concentrate on it."

Tina Louise has learned to ignore her shaking hands and knees.

"I let them shake as much as they like," she admitted to us. "I tell myself they don't shake off and eventually they stop."

Meanwhile she evokes the sensation allowing sunlight to bathe her body until a feeling warmth begins to reach her taut muscles.

Carroll Baker forgets her tension and concentrates instead on what she must do. Thus she is able to channel her nervous energy into constructive uses.

Men seem to prefer a more active form of relieving tensions. Jack Palance likes to run round the sound stage until he has used up his excess energy and is relaxed enough to play his scenes.

Tony Curtis does vigorous physical exercises, such as pushups, with the same results.

But rather than recommend pushups or other such stunts, we pass along these exercises for relaxation and balanced tension, which drama coach Estelle Harman teachcs her students.

Exercise 1

Choose a comfortable chair, sit down and close your eyes. Then ask yourself this question, "Am I comfortable?"

Be thorough about it. Begin by asking specifically of each part of your anatomy, "Are you comfortable, neck? Shoulders, are you comfortable? Rib cage?" Don't just ask the question—ask it expecting an answer, and listen carefully. If you find the least tension in any of these parts, pause to relax it before moving on.

Finally you will be able to claim that you are truly comfortable in every way. By that time you may be sprawled out like a rag doll in the chair Having reached this ultimate degree of relaxation, pause for a few minutes to enjoy it.

Then begin to pull yourself back in shape again by waking, one by one, the parts of your body with the question, "What tension happened then to you, leg?" You examine the tension. If you find it too strong for comfort, relax it slightly.

Moving over your body in this way, you will presently find yourself in a position which is neither slovenly or tense. Everything will feel comfortable but at the same time alert and ready for action. This is the state of balanced tension. A little practice will help you become familiar with it.

Exercise 2

Stretch your body at full tension with your arms raised over your head. Stretch, stretch, stretch, as though you were reaching for the moon. Now you are on your tip-toes, all of your body straining tautly upward. Hold it a minute in that position.

Then you begin to relax gradually, starting with your fingertips. Relax your fingers, your wrists, your arms, your head, shoulders, torso, legs, feet.

On your way down, pause to take special note of the in-between position when you're no longer in tension but are not yet completely relaxed. This too is the position of balanced tension.

Once you have recognized it and enjoyed it for a second, continue downward. Feel yourself turning into rubber, growing more and more limp as you crumple to the floor. Now your arms are swinging lifelessly, your head drops forward, your body is hunched over like an ape's. And still more and more until finally you crumple like silk to the door. This movement not only gives you the feel of balanced tension but also enables you to compare it with that of complete relaxation.

Actors, by the way, use this exercise to prepare themselves for stage falls without injury.

six

Emotion

FEELING: MAGIC KEY NUMBER FOUR

HAVE you ever given a speech that you thought was perfect, and yet it didn't move anyone? On the other hand, have you ever made a few apparently insignificant remarks that, to your surprise, stirred people deeply? What causes the difference? The answer—feeling.

The success of many professions literally depends on feeling. Dr. Rex Kennamer, Well-known Hollywood physician, gives feeling a prominent place among a doctor's tools. He believes the very meaning of the word "physician" is one who feels for his patient, in contrast to the medical scientist who has only an abstract interest in the disease itself.

"Of course, anyone who enters our profession has to learn all there is to know about medicine," he told us. "But over and above this, we in the healing arts really should be physicians and not scientists."

The great trial lawyers are those who present their cases with feeling. The most successful politicians know how to evoke it in their constituents. Public speakers from the President of the United States to the businessman before the Rotary Club are the better for the use of feeling in their delivery.

The minister, the rabbi and the priest waken the best in us by appealing to our emotions as well as to our intellects. They know that to be emotionally rich you must be able to give freely of yourself.

WHY FEELING?

Gertrude Fogler, the great Hollywood voice coach who was formerly an actress, explained it to us this way:

"Meaning comes from the mind, but you can't put meaning across without emotion, and emotion comes from the solar plexus behind your diaphragm. If you hear good news, it is as though a light shone warmly there. If you receive bad news, it is as though someone had struck you with a fist in the same place."

Emotion makes such an impact on us because our reactions to it are located in the solar plexus and not in the mind. We respond immediately and in kind to the emotion people radiate. Hate wakens hate; love wins friends. Enthusiasm convinces and brings victory to "lost" causes. When a man asks for a raise, and can in the process stir up a spark of friendship or compassion or enthusiasm in his employer, the battle is usually won.

Even the most pedestrian job may be energized by adding a feeling of love. The man who is enthusiastic about his job will enrich it and enlarge it, and consequently will provide a contribution to his society and will himself move on to broader horizons. Nothing in the world so inspires confidence in a person's abilities as the warmth he brings to living.

ACTORS AND FEELING

Being able to feel their roles is a prerequisite with actors. Yet they, like most of us, have frequently allowed their feeling antennae to become dulled. This does not apply to emotion alone, but to the elemental bodily sensations that made life so exciting to us as children.

Therefore, most drama coaches begin by retraining their young students to feel "organically" again.

What is meant by feeling "organically"? To understand it think back over the observation exercises you've been practicing. Have you been observing only with your eyes? Then you have been making merely a partial contact with life.

Perhaps you have brought into play the senses of hearing and smelling. What about taste and touch as well?

Here are the instructions Bob Gist, well-known drama coach, actor and director, gives his beginners to sharpen their awareness of the sensory centers.

"Learn to listen not only to what others are saying, but also to how they are saying it. Really taste every morsel of food and drink that passes your lips. Get the individual smells of things. Awaken to the feel of wind or rain or sun on your body. Get acquainted with life as you experienced it in childhood."

TRY IT YOURSELF

If you have been following the suggestions in Chapter 4, "Your physical Apparatus," you will have grown more aware of your body as something you are living in and not simply with. Now try using the body, as the young drama student is taught to do, as an agent to contact all physical phases of the outside world. Become aware of everything you see, hear, smell, taste or touch and try to describe honestly the sensation each object you so "observe" rouses within you.

The store of information you pick up from the senses will aid you in evaluating people and situations more accurately.

The man with whom you are preparing to do business and who appears so honest may reveal himself as a dangerous partner by the picture your mind is able to construct out of the whole of your sensory observations. This is because your careful and minute attention to such data has given your intuition a concise sensory picture on which to base its "feeling" judgements.

There is nothing magical about intuition. It is regularly practiced by primitive peoples whose safety depends on their sensory perceptions and who therefore have developed them to a very high degree.

Look at your conscious mind as a gigantic computer machine. The more information you feed into it, the more accurate will be the resultant analysis. We will go into this subject in greater detail in Chapter 9, "The Art of Human Understanding".

FOLLOWING THE ACTOR-BUT NOT ALL THE WAY

As the young actor increases his ability to live organically and to voice his own unique reactions to his feelings, he moves on to the next step, the "uncorking" of his emotions.

Learning how to "let go" at appropriate times is necessary for an actor, because during his career he must play a variety of roles that run the gamut of emotions. He cannot depict these emotions authentically unless he is acquainted with them from first-hand experience.

We attended several "uncorking" classes for beginning students conducted by Tony Barr, coach at the Alexander-Barr school of acting. His classes are typical of those held by the finest drama coaches in Hollywood.

Since the young student must eventually display his emotions before an audience, one of Barr's exercises requires that the student act out these emotions on the stage before his classmates. The emotions—fear, anger, hatred, love, joy, and so on—are taken up in turn and each is demonstrated over and over by the individual student, until finally genuine feeling begins to break through.

At first, students react with artificial cliches that do not convey realism since they come from the mind rather than the solar plexus. It is only when they learn to go back to some previous experience, during which they sincerely felt the emotion, and relive it to the full, that this emotion can break to the surface.

WE CAN TAKE A LESSON

We actors on the stage of life, unlike our counterparts in the theater, are not called upon to change our roles frequently. Therefore we have no need to dig out of ourselves the proper expressions for the whole gamut of emotions.

Life, unlike the casting directors of stage, screen and television, gives each of us the opportunity to create as well as play our own parts. Unless we wish to do so, there is no need for us to play negative or hateful roles on the stage of life.

By following the actor's methods we can create for ourselves a vibrant positive personality. Perhaps at first, if we have been in the habit of indulging our darker and more depressing emotions, it will not be easy. Yet with a little effort it can be done.

Just as the beginner in an acting school is instructed to think back to some experience in which he felt the emotion he is supposed to portray, so you can recapture the lost emotion of, say, enthusiasm, by looking back into the past for a moment when you felt it strongly. All of us have known such moments from time to time, no matter how fleeting they may have been or how transitory the object that aroused them. Your enthusiasm as a schoolchild over a class picnic, for example, can be more potent than many of your adult enthusiasms.

When you recall such a moment of strong emotion in your life, don't regard it as an insignificant childhood event. Instead, enlarge on it by reconstructing it down to the last detail.

Try especially to recapture your **feelings** of that day. You will be helped by concentrating on such sensory perceptions as how the woods looked, how the joyful voices of your classmates struck your ear and how the soft moss felt under your feet.

As these feelings are recaptured in the frame of that experience they will flood over into the present, moving out of the field of mental memory into your solar plexus. Then you will find yourself in possession of a store of positive energy to apply to the chores of the day.

UTILIZE THE FUTURE, TOO

Some actors, and you can be one of them, don't look into the past for an occasion that will rouse enthusiasm—they look into the future. They think of some coming project for which they have great enthusiasm and allow the feeling to engulf them. They then channel it into the distasteful task at hand.

Think, for instance, of the exciting vacation you are planning. Be sure to **feel** what you will be doing. Finally use the energy created by that **feeling** to take care of the chores at hand. Remind yourself that these distasteful chores are providing the money which will enable you to take this vacation.

THOSE EXPLOSIVE EMOTIONS

Enthusiasm, joy, love and similar positive emotions bring with them an all-around sense of well-being, for they are toners of the body as well as the mind. The same cannot be said of the destructive emotions, such as anger, depression, doubt and fear.

Negative feelings come to all of us from time to time. They not only darken our day, they make us unattractive to our fellow men and cause us to perform badly, sometimes with serious consequences, on the stage of life.

Ill-timed flareups, whatever the provocation, can spoil important human relationships and often ruin pending business deals. Anger clouds judgment. Fear in the shape of panic at times of disaster causes more deaths than the disaster itself.

A leading Los Angeles cardiologist told us of a man who suffered a mild heart attack and called on a doctor friend for help. The doctor, who had not properly trained his own emotions, went to pieces. His hysterical behavior convinced the patient that he was on the verge of death. This terror induced such a state of panic in the patient that the sedative had no effect whatsoever.

The patient might have died, not of the mild heart attack, but of fear and shock if the doctor who cited this case hadn't taken on the job of quieting his fears and giving him encouragement.

A NEUTRALIZATION SECRET

The question is, then, how to close the barn door before, instead of after, the horse gets out. The late Dr. Margaret Steger, student of the famous Swiss psychiatrist and psychoanalyst Dr. Carl Gustav Jung and herself a prominent Viennese psychologist, gave us this exercise for neutralizing harmful emotions. It is a variation in reverse of the method actors use to **arouse** feeling.

During a period of calm and relaxation choose a sensory-motor occupation with which you are familiar because you have performed it many times before. It may be rowing boat, scrubbing a floor, digging in the garden, driving, swimming, dancing. But it must have this one attribute—the occupation must never have been distasteful to you.

Feel yourself into this occupation, being careful not to confine yourself to a visual presentation alone. Get so into the feel of it that you are actually **doing** it in your imagination. You will then experience a quiet, neutral emotion, the emotion that comes when we are performing something pleasant though monotonous.

Now, when a destructive emotion strikes you—concentrate on the neutral emotion you've been practicing. By neutralizing your mind before filling it with a positive emotion, you avoid the risk of simply repressing your anger where it will work against you in undercurrents of anxiety and resentment.

After you have neutralized the destructive emotion, **then** radiate yourself with the positive emotion—whether enthusiasm, courage, confidence—that will best help you to solve the dilemma of the moment.

RADIATION

It was the late Michael Chekhov who first formulated the method he called radiation. His use of it enabled him to become. a sensitive and convincing actor. Later as an instructor he taught the method to his pupils. Since then many drama coaches have instructed their pupils in the use of this radiation principle.

One of the dictionary definitions of the verb "to radiate" from which the noun "radiation" is taken, is: "To issue in rays as light or heat." Chekhov applied this definition to his radiation principle in acting.

He maintained that with practice it was possible to emit rays or waves of emotion into the surrounding atmosphere just as potently in the psychological realm as the energized sun emits rays of light in the physical. These rays of emotion, he firmly believed, could communicate themselves to others without the use of gesture or word.

Charles Leonard, Chekhov's close associate, tells the following story which was related to him by a famous Broadway actor. One day this actor, then unknown, asked Chekhov to take him as his pupil. During the course of the interview Chekhov brought up his novel theory of radiation.

"I believe, Jack, that you can sit in your chair and radiate almost any emotion to a person without moving a muscle or a finger," he said. "Love, hate, fear, suspicion, anger, self-confidence, and that person will get it."

The actor stared at him dubiously. He didn't believe a word of what he regarded as an outlandish theory. Before Chekhov had a chance to explain himself the phone in the next room rang. He was gone for almost fifteen minutes. Then he hurried back to apologize to his guest.

On the threshold of the room he stopped short, shocked. The air was charged with animosity.

"What's wrong, Jack?" he exclaimed. "What's happened? You're angry about something. Tell me what it is. I'm sure it's just a misunderstanding I can explain to you:"

At his words the actor laughed.

"Oh, no, I'm not angry," he said. "I was just putting your radiation theory to the test. It does work."

HOW TO PRACTICE RADIATION

If you are interested in experimenting with the magic skill of radiation, practice this exercise. It is a variation of those taught by Chekhov and other farsighted drama coaches. It requires the use of your imagination and some relaxation of your intellect in favor of your emotion, for this is an exercise of pure feeling.

Stand in the center of your room. Look inside yourself. See and feel the life coursing through you. See your body energized with life just as the sun is energized with heat and light.

Lift your arm and **feel** that energized life sweeping up it in rays of light. Feel those rays channeling themselves through your outstretched fingers and on into the room beyond you. Lift your other arm and send out more rays from it. These rays may be pictured in the form of pulsating waves of light, but you must be sure to **feel** as well as to see them.

The exercise isn't so hard to do once you realize that life is coursing through you all the time, and you are only now becoming aware of its great potentialities.

Imagine the rays pouring out of your head, your thighs, knees, feet. Imagine yourself surrounded by them. If you can conjure up a visual picture of a scintillating aura of living rays completely encircling you, so much the better. But always strive for the **feel** as well as the image of the aura.

Now with your imagination, stretch that aura wider and wider by allowing more life force to pour out of yourself. Fill the whole room with it. Make it sparkle in every nook and cranny. However always remain conscious of yourself as the core and the source of that pulsating sea of rays.

Finally, gather the rays back into yourself and feel them concentrated and vibrating with light within you. Send them out again as before and again withdraw them. Practice this in a kind of rhythmic movement several times whenever you have a few free moments. Make a game of it.

Once you possess the electric **feel** of radiation itself, you can begin radiating certain qualities and emotions. Radiate in turn enthusiasm, love, joy, peace. If you have been resurrecting these emotions from childhood experiences, you will have become acquainted firsthand with the actual feeling they rouse in you.

Radiation will enable you to magnify that **feeling** many times:

TRY IT IN COLOR

To make your radiation even more potent, think in **terms of color** of the different emotion-rays that you evoke in your body and pour out to fill the room.

To discover just how much color influences your emotions, try this experiment. Illuminate your room with varicolored light bulbs, or look at the world through colored pieces of cellophane; note the different reactions you have to each color.

You will then realize how potently color affects you. In fact, the influence colors have on our emotions was tested at the Lumiere, a French film factory in Lyons. When red lighting was used the workers behaved in a highly excitable manner. They sang, gesticulated and tended to be high-strung in general. By night they were worn out.

When green lighting was used, the employees went at their work in a far calmer manner. At closing time they were still rested enough to enjoy a night on the town.

At least one coach, David Alexander, makes use of color to train his students.

"We found that not only the physical response of actors varies decidedly when associated with different colors, but that even the tone of their voices is affected," he told us. "If I were to say to one of my students, for instance, 'Play the scene in red,' and then, 'Play it in white,' you would see at once how differently it would be done."

No less an authority than the late Dr. C. G. Jung accorded color a prominent place in stimulating the unconscious. He encouraged his patients to paint in color. If you can think in color, therefore, your radiation will be that much more potent.

Here is a brief list depicting colors as they are commonly felt by people.

Shades of red ate physical feeling rousers

Shades of yellow are stimulants of mental enthusiasm

Shades of green are harmony-creating

Shades of blue rouse spiritual qualities

Shades of purple combine spiritual with physical qualities of feeling.

If you react to colors in ways that differ from the chart above, however, follow your own interpretation. But remember that the more vivid the color the purer the emotion. Dull colors are depressants.

Once you decide to make use of the ally of color, try this exercise as a starter. Radiate a sense of urgency by seeing brilliant scarlet rays filling your body and pouring out to engulf the entire room. Standing in the core of these gleaming blood-red rays, perform certain simple acts such as walking, sitting, moving arms and head.

Next, flood yourself and surroundings with cool blue shades and make the same movements. Notice how different your responses are to the change of color.

Faithfully practice these radiation exercises and presently you will be able to energize your entire being with any emotion or quality necessary to face a particular crisis or event in your life. Don't be discouraged if your responses are weak at first. Constant repetition and belief in what you are doing will eventually enable you to match every mental idea with a fitting solar plexus response.

Here are exercises to enable you to make a closer acquaintance with your feeling propensities, so that you may use them in your performances on the stage of life.

EXERCISE 1 **An exercise used by Stanislavski for developing sensory reaction among his students**

Choose some object that you can handle. Observe it carefully for thirty seconds, first with your eyes, and jot down your observations of it.

Next take the same object in your hands. Feel it, smell it, examine it closely with your hands. Spend thirty seconds on using both hands and eyes and then record your observations. This exercise will show you how, by becoming totally involved with anything, you become more deeply aware of it.

EXERCISE 2 **An exercise given by Stanislavski for training emotional awareness of his pupils**

When you go to bed at night review your whole day in sequence, starting from the last thing you did and moving backward. Bring everything that happened sharply to mind. But do not make this review an intellectual act alone. Get the feel, the smell the taste of everything that took place.

Sometimes, instead of reviewing the day, try to call up the faces of friends and acquaintances, either of recent years or of bygone times. Do not make this an intellectual exercise of memory, but try to evoke the feeling you experienced formerly at the sight of each face.

EXERCISE 3 **An exercise for radiating joy after Michael Chekhov's radiation method**

We have selected the emotion of joy for this exercise because. according to Tony Barr, it is the most difficult one for modern man to resurrect from his unconscious. At the same time it is the most magically endowed to attract others and to give us personal well-being.

First try to recapture the feelings you had as a child when experiencing some joyous event. It need be no more significant then the sound of the ice-cream man's bell on a hot day and the delicious taste of his ice-cream.

When you have captured even a little of these feelings translate them into the sparkling gold of pure sunshine. Fee l that golden light radiating through your whole body. Increase its intensity by radiating the stream of light into a great tide. Pour this golden tide outward from you in all directions. See it surrounding you in a sparkling aura scintillating with millions of dazzling flakes.

Bathe yourself in that aura. You will be delighted with the potent feeling of well-being that fills you.

Now practice a rich belly laugh for good measure. There is nothing so infectious as wholehearted laughter for establishing good relationships with others. Yet how rarely you hear it. Most of the time we get no more then a self conscious deprecating chuckle.

EXERCISE 4 **An exercise for wholehearted laughter that comes from Zina Provendie**

Go into a room where you will be alone. Draw a deep breathe through your mouth into the diaphragm which lies just below your rib cage. When it has expanded like a balloon, begin to deflate it by releasing your breath through your mouth in a series of Ha! Ha! Ha's!

Don't worry about its sounding artificial. Just concentrate on those sounds.

Next begin your ha-ha-ha's in a low key, but as you let them out raise each one to a key above its predecessor.

After you have practiced a while, try giving ha-ha-ha's up and down the scale. Make them louder. Abandon yourself completely even if you have to force yourself to do so.

The secret is not to allow yourself time to feel self-conscious.

Finally, see all these ha-ha-ha's radiating light themselves. Your laughter should now have the rich ring of spontaneity.

One last suggestion. Once you have cultivated laughter, don't be afraid to open your throat and let it out whenever the impulse strikes you. The world has enough of gloom. It can use every bit of wholehearted laughter.

seven

Imagination

IMAGINATION: MAGIC KEY NUMBER FIVE

ARE you in the habit of dreaming about what you'd like to do or who you'd like to be? Good! Dreams can be turned into active imagination—the magic key to help you play your role as you wish it to be played. The man without a dream is one who plays a narrow, colorless role in life, makes few friends and wonders why the excitement and joy of living seem to have passed him by.

If you believe that you must see, touch, taste or smell something before it has reality, why not start changing this at once? Even if you don't believe in the effect of dreams on life, just try it as a kind of silly game. We'll guarantee a transformation in your life—once you give your dreams a chance to break through.

ARE YOUR DREAMS NEGATIVE?

Some of us possess enough of imagination, but we use it in the wrong way. Instead of counting our blessings, we tote up our misfortunes. We wake up to the sun with the expectation of a storm by noon. We embark on a business deal with the expectation of failure. We see catastrophe looming in every minor event of the day. We relate a long rigamarole of illness, disappointment and business failure every time someone asks us how we are.

However if you are one of these people, congratulate yourself.

You have a vivid imagination. All you need do is to train it in the right course. Do this and it will just as certainly bring you all the good things you've wanted but felt could never be yours because you were under a cloud of "ill luck."

This is because the "ill luck" that seems to haunt us from birth to death is usually a creation of our own vivid imaginations. Our unconscious is a faithful servant. It takes up any picture we present to it and proceeds to bring it into reality. It helps us throw up the roadblocks which we believe come from external sources. It puts a negative cast on our relations with others. It works in every way to prove to us that we really are children of "ill luck."

Once you learn how, you can as vividly "will" good luck upon yourself. All you have to do is present a vibrant picture of success to your unconscious. It will work just as faithfully to bring it into reality as it did before with your bad luck picture.

TRAINING YOUR IMAGINATION

Bob Cummings suggests the following method for transforming your negative imagination into a positive one.

Take a little time each night to do what motion picture directors do every day while their picture is in progress. They sit down in a projection room and run all the footage they shot that day—"rushes," as they're called—to see how the picture is progressing and to select the best from among them for the finished film.

Sit or lie down yourself and imagine you are a projection machine, The rushes you're about to be showing are ones in which you are the star performer. They comprise the story of your day's activities. And the screen on which they will be thrown is the screen of life.

Now start looking at these rushes. Do they show you as a dynamic, forceful person, a person who knows that he is about and sets out positively to achieve it? Or do you see, instead, a timid, disorientated person who gives the impression of being uncertain about his role in life and how it should be played?

If so, select from among the day's activities several of the most telling incidents, Now deliberately project them on the screen of life as you would have liked to see them played. Do this with feeling, remembering that you have two alternatives open to you at all times-one positive, one negative. The mental picture which you choose to slip in just behind your eyes is the one that eventually will be projected into life.

Practice correcting your rushes in this way everyday for a while and you will presently become aware of a steady transformation for the better in the role you are playing on the stage of life. You will find, too, that people respond positively to your new dynamic personality and that you are offered opportunities in keeping with your newly expanded role.

IMAGINATION CAN CREATE **THINGS,** TOO

Imagination not only improves your role in life, it also has the power to attract the scenery against which that role can be performed most satisfactorily. For imagination can produce physical changes.

Here is how a young girl we know made imagination work for her. She loved a tasteful home, but when she went to New York she was compelled to live in a small, cramped apartment.

She could afford little in the way of dressing up the apartment so she decided to furnish it with the warmth of her imagination.

"You are my home," she told it. "When I return tired from a long day's work you give me shelter and rest. I see you as a sanctuary."

When friends came to visit her she welcomed them graciously into the little apartment. She never spoke of its inconveniences but only of its advantages. Through her eyes the visitors saw a fascinating "view" from her window. The prints from the dime store that hung on the walls and the inexpensive little odds and ends which she'd bought with loving care seemed to give a special air of taste and friendless. Somehow the apartment seemed to expand. No one thought of t as a cramped, dark place.

Some of her friends were envious and said so. Others voiced the wish that they could find a similar apartment. No one even guessed that it was all the product of just a little imagination:

Then an interesting thing began to happen. Suddenly people wanted to have a share in the apartment. A friend who was moving and didn't have room in the new place brought several fine pictures to hang in it. Someone else who took a trip abroad found some quaint pieces for the bric-a-brac shelf. Another admirer brought home a charming ivory statuette from Hong Kong for the stand beside the door.

Presently the apartment really became a tasteful and charming place in which to live.

Imagination works like that. It expands on the physical as well as the mental plane, because on either plane it has the power to attract to itself more and more of whatever you have evoked, whether of good or bad.

LET YOUR IMAGINATION WRITE YOUR SCENES

If you have known the disappointment of seeing a fine idea or a favorite project rejected, ask yourself if the fault may have lain in not having presented it dramatically enough to attract attention. An imaginative presentation often saves the day for a great idea that might otherwise have been tossed aside.

When the need for a dramatic presentation arises for the professional actor he looks to his knapsack of odds and ends collected through careful observation, and from among them he selects those ingredients that will make his action come alive. Many creative people in the film colony have learned that by using the same kind of imaginative creative selection in real life they can play a more convincing role and achieve their goals. They can have fun doing it, too, because creating a scene is a form of play.

Colonel Tom Parker, Elvis Presley's manager, began his present career by handling a troupe of country folk singers. The performers had caught the attention of the heads of a big record company from the East. With four lawyers in tow they went to Nashville, Tennessee, to sign up the singers.

Colonel Parker didn't have the money then to hire a lawyer, but he put an even more valuable asset—his imagination—to work to help him get a fair deal for his singers.

He decided to create his own lawyer. He remembered a bass fiddle player with an imposing front. He told the man to wear a broadbrimmed hat and to carry a large black cigar in the corner of his mouth. His instructions were to sit still and watch his employer. Whenever the Colonel looked at him he was to set his jaws, frown and shake his head slowly back and forth.

By using this phony lawyer, who shook his head at every cue, Colonel Parker was able to persuade the smart lawyers from the East to set up a fabulous deal for his singers.

He succeeded because he wasn't afraid to gamble with his imagination.

SIMPLE WAYS TO ATTRACT ATTENTION

There are just about as many ways to dramatize an idea or a product as there are individuals. You will have to look into your own knapsack to see what combinations you can form out of what you find there. Remember, the more observations you have gathered the better able you will be to create a drama that will aid you in achieving your goal.

You will discover that in most instances elaborate dramas are unnecessary. The following examples will give you an idea of what can be done by using just a little Imagination.

THE IMAGINATIVE TIRE SALESMAN

Back in Depression days Ivan Stauffer, now head of public relations and the travel department under Howard Strickling at M-G-M Studios, was working as a filling station operator. The oil company that employed him decided to pep up its tire sales by offering a trip to Europe to the employee who could sell the most tires.

This was an unheard of bonus in those days, and Stauffer, a young man at the time, was determined to win that free trip. So he composed the following little play which he acted out from house to house in Beverly Hills.

First he would give a long sharp pull at the doorbell.

When the owner of the house answered, Stauffer would say, "Sir, is that your car out there? If so, I wanted to warn you there's four bombs under it."

The man, taken by surprise, would run out to examine his car at the curb. Ivan would follow him and, pointing at the tires, would say, "Sir, I mean your tires. I notice the treads are getting worn. If they blow out on the highway you may be in as great danger as if they were real bombs."

By using this imaginative approach Stauffer was able to far outsell all of his competitors and win the free trip to Europe.

THE IMAGINARY TOOTHACHE

Here's another little imaginative drama used by Rick Carrier, the director, to sell a story idea to producer Joe Levine.

Levine was very busy at the time and Carrier was afraid he would give only half an ear to his idea unless he could draw full attention to himself. He did so by imagining a toothache so vividly that his face became contorted with suffering. This roused Levine's sympathy and he listened attentively while Carrier described his idea.

The result of Carrier's imaginative little drama was that he made a successful sale.

CHANGING ROLES

We now come to the person—perhaps it's you.-who wants to get into different work and doesn't know how to go about it.

Here's the little drama Bob Cummings played to get into the acting profession.

At the time he wanted to follow this career there was a craze for young British leading men. Without an English accent it was almost impossible to get an acting job. Cummings beat the pavements in New York fruitlessly, visiting agency after agency and being rejected by every one.

Then one day when he was completely down and out he came into a modest windfall. His mother sent him several hundred dollars from an insurance policy she had taken out on him when he was a baby. It was the heart of the Depression and money was scarce. So the several hundred dollars represented real riches.

Most people would have horded it carefully. Not Bob! He decided to use it to help him play a little drama which could enable him to become an actor.

First he came upon an advertisement that offered a round trip to England by boat for only 135 dollars. He bought a ticket and was off. He spent twenty-nine days in England studying until he had the British accent down to a "T". Then he changed his name to something that would attract real attention-Blade Stanhope Conway.

One day in a small English town he saw a man changing the marquee on a theater. He paid out some of his fast-dwindling resources to have the man put up the name of Blade Stanhope Conway in lights. Then he took a picture of the marquee and had the workman snap one of him while he stood under it.

He returned to New York with the pictures, a new name and a British accent so thick you could slice it with a knife. As a "well-known" British actor he now was desirable and within three days had landed the lead in John Galsworthy's **The Roof.** From then on his career moved forward rapidly and soon he could drop both his British accent and his fictitious name and succeed as himself with his own real talent.

BUT HOW ABOUT YOU?

Perhaps you are saying at this point that it is all very well for Bob Cummings, a young man without family ties or responsibilities, to go flying off to the ends of the earth to make his dream come true. But you have a wife and children to support and can't afford to take such risks.

But risks aren't necessary. Here are a few simple rules you can follow right at home and at your present job to help you improve your position.

First, start looking at that job in a constructive way. Make a list of its redeeming qualities. There must be one, at least—it is providing you and your family with food and shelter.

After you've learned to look at the job you have in a constructive way, try to form a clear picture of what you really want out of life. You may be surprised at how muddled and vague your ideas are about this. You have spent so much time complaining about the present that you've never even stopped to ask yourself how you might change the future to make it more pleasant for you.

Once you get your picture clear and begin to dwell on it positively, your imagination will find all sorts of ways to help you take advantage of your present circumstances to bring you toward your goal.

THREE RULES

In transforming your daydreams into active imagination three basic ingredients are necessary.

1. Clarity of your basic picture
2. Belief in your goal
3. Enthusiasm

CLARITY

Before you can bring your imaginative picture into reality you must be able to see clearly what you want. Do you, for instance, want to work at a certain profession for its own sake? Or because you believe that it will bring you money, fame and social position?

If the second is so, you must understand clearly that your interest is not in the profession at all but in the fruits that you believe it will bring you. If you are interested only in these fruits then you must concentrate on them alone and let the profession which will bring them to you take care of itself.

But remember this: The greater good your mental picture promises to those around you the greater weight it will carry in your own mind. This is how the human psyche works. It is simply that more expanded vision brings with it a more expanded energy. There is nothing strange about it. It is a psychological law.

BELIEF

Once you have made a clear picture of what you want, you must believe in the possibility of its becoming reality. And this belief must be so strong that you will be able to ignore all the obstacles that may lie between you and its fulfilments.

The Honorable Cecil Bennett, dynamic Premier of British Columbia who has won more elections and held his high office longer than any other leader in the history of the province, sums it up this way, "The spoils belong to the man with glittering sword."

That glittering sword, to our way of thinking, is the sword of belief in one's goal, though the goal itself need not be right or worthy.

"This is the secret of a confidence man's success," says Gordon Gordon, ex-FBI agent who, with his wife Mildred, turns out such best-selling mystery novels as **Operation Terror** and **Undercover Cat.**

"He studies the part he is going to play so thoroughly that by the time he begins working on his victim it isn't a swindle to him any longer. It's a legitimate business deal. This is why he can take in his victims by the most obvious get-rich-quick schemes."

ENTHUSIASM

It is not enough to see your basic picture and to have belief in it. You must be enthusiastic about achieving it as well. Enthusiasm is the ingredient that gives imagination the impetus which differentiates it from passive daydreaming. Daydreaming has no power to perpetuate itself beyond the moment's duration, even though the picture is clarified and the belief strong. Active Imagination, on the other hand, is imagination **energized** by enthusiasm.

"It's like electricity," Bob Gist says. "Nobody really knowns what it is but it works—either for you or against you. If you seek it hard enough it will always answer you, and positively as long as you're in key with life."

All professional actors realize the importance of developing this magical tool of imagination and work at it daily. Here are some of the exercises they follow. These exercises resemble play more than work. They're great for relaxation as well as for improving imagination. Best of all, they can send you back to the fairyland of childhood where you woke each morning with the firm belief that something exciting was going to happen to you during the day—and because you expected it, it usually did.

EXERCISE 1 **A game the late Michael Chekhov used to play**

Chekhov used to have two pets from which he was inseparable. One was a stuffed lion and the other a stuffed monkey. In almost every moment of his spare time he would carry on animated conversations with these two stuffed animals, imagining their responses to him in turn. He even dreamed up little skits, inventing characterizations and situations for himself and his two pets to perform.

A variation Bob Gist, M-G-M director who has done many of the Dr. Kildare TV shows, actor and drama coach, goes a step farther. With the magic wand of his imagination he transforms any inanimate object he chooses into something alive and whimsical. In this quick metamorphosis an ash tray may suddenly sprout an imaginary tail, long jaws full of sharp teeth, stubby legs and a scaly back.

Gist begins to carry on a conversation with this little creature, which, gifted with energy from his imagination, no longer appears to be an inanimate thing, but has the power to dart here and there. It returns his interest with friendship and replies when he asks it a question.

The fact that the object's answers are Gist's own often brings out of Gist's unconscious a wealth of buried observation that enables him to perform more imaginatively in his roles.

Psychologists recommend this kind of play as a form of getting acquainted with oneself. It tends to draw hidden resources into the open and make them available for use.

EXERCISE 2 **An exercise in pantomime for increasing the imagination by Estelle Harman**

Take a simple object, say a dime-store ash tray. Assume it is an art object from the Ming Dynasty and handle it as though it were. Treat it with care and admiration, turning it round and round in your hands to get the delicacy of line, the exquisite colors, the intricate design and so forth.

Then put the object down and repeat the same scene in pantomime, trying to make the imaginary object with all its rare attributes come alive in your hands. If you don't feel it is really there, go back to handling the object again to see what you have missed.

Keep practicing until you actually have the feel of the object and can give a realistic representation of it, drawing only on your store of imagination.

EXERCISE 3 **An exercise from Stanislavski**

If you have been studying some country as was suggested in Chapter 2, "Observation," set about making an imaginary trip to that country. Sit down every evening and feel yourself with as much realism as possible into the scenes about which you have been reading. Get the smells, sounds, taste and feel of things as well as the pictorial sights.

You will discover that the more you abandon yourself to this imaginative journey the more real it will become for you. Eventually, if you have used your imagination strongly enough, it will draw to itself the situations and opportunity which will enable you to repeat the journey in the flesh. But that will only be a practical result. The exercise should be done primarily to develop your imagination.

eight

Rhythm and Atmosphere

THE IMPORTANCE OF RHYTHM

WE SELDOM realize how important rhythm is in playing roles correctly on the stage of life or what an ally it can be if understood and properly used.

Yet unconscious recognition of the vital importance of rhythm is reflected in such phrases as "I felt out of step with the times," or "Somehow we couldn't synchronize," or "I couldn't get into the swing of it."

Rhythms can be used to help us display our emotions physically, mentally and emotionally. In fact, rhythms can be used to engender the emotion we wish to display at any given time or to simulate it realistically.

PROFESSIONAL ACTORS AND THE SECRET OF RHYTHMS

Professional actors who have to display a "true" emotion night after night, often for months at a time, discover that they cannot always rely on inner inspiration to bring reality to the scene When this happens they MUST have some gimmick to rouse or simulate the necessary emotion. Rhythm serves as a wonderful device to help them achieve their end.

DO YOU NEED TO BORROW AN EMOTION?

Perhaps there are moments when you need to borrow the rhythm of an emotion not genuinely fell to help you over a crisis. A display of anger or righteous indignation, for instance, may be necessary to get the cooperation of some recalcitrant employee or to confront some dangerous situation that could spell your ruin. Yet to stir yourself deliberately to a high pitch of anger could be self-destructive, as anger has a tendency to cloud judgment.

EMOTIONS CAN BE SIMULATED

Producer Ross Hunter makes frank use of simulated emotions. During the shooting of a picture, one of his stars refused to play a scene as he wanted it played. To get the star to cooperate Hunter went into the rhythms of anger, demanding that she obey.

"She was so scared I was going to bust a gasket that she did what I asked like a lamb," he recalled for us, laughing, "But actually I couldn't have been more calm inside."

In a more serious crisis Hunter called upon the rhythms of a good humor he did not feel to help him get through a crisis. He was in the middle of shooting a picture when he received news that his mother had died. Though his mind was in a turmoil of grief he knew he must not reveal his feelings to the cast.

By using the rhythms of good humor he was able to keep up a simulated cheer during shooting hours. As a result he was able to turn out a successful comedy.

PRACTICING EMOTION RHYTHMS

You can learn the same trick by trying the following. It is one of a series of exercises that David Alexander gives his drama students to acquaint them with the physical rhythms of various emotions.

First fling your arm out forcefully, your finger pointing emphatically and say, "Get out!" You will find the gesture of your arm has lent strength to your voice. In fact, it has even sent a slight stir of adrenaline through your blood stream. This kind of gesture is known as a psychological gesture, and its purpose is to trigger the rhythms of the mood you wish to capture.

To continue your experiment, fold your head in your arms, allow your shoulders to sag, and say, "Get out" again. In that posture your voice will automatically shed its authority and take on a despairing, almost hopeless tinge. Every bodily posture you initiate will bring coloration of the mood it expresses to your voice.

TEMPO

Now go through the gamut of emotions, physicalizing them as you do. Ask yourself the exact feeling you experience in the process. Thus you will not only know the broad emotional categories but you will also be able to distinguish the more subtle nuances of each emotion.

An important discovery you will make is that the rate of speed at which you perform your psychological gestures determines the type as well as the content of the emotion you are trying to simulate.

For instance, to perform the psychological gestures of anger in high speed is to give the impression of being a spitfire. To perform the same psychological gesture slowly is to give the impression of a stern, cold fury.

Similarly take an emotion of well-being—such as happiness. To make the rhythmic gestures of happiness slowly and calmly is to give the impression of contentment; to execute them swiftly is to give the impression of joy.

After you have practiced simulating the rhythms of emotions you will discover that when the emotion itself is not available you can use its rhythms to put across your meaning.

OTHER USES OF PHYSICALIZED RHYTHMS

You will also discover that, if you let yourself go, you can use these physicalized rhythms to stir a desired emotion into being.

This is because, as Stanislavski often told his pupils, "The bond between body and soul is indivisible. The life of the one gives life to the other. Every physical act, except simply mechanical ones, has an inner source of feeling."

You can readily prove the truth of this statement. When you are depressed try this curative formula, suggested by Tony Barr, for lightening your spirits.

Depression is a dark, destructive emotion with slow, almost static rhythms. When you are afflicted by it concentrate on physicalizing the rapid rhythms of its opposite number, joy.

Do everything at a fast tempo. Go for a walk and walk briskly. If possible, run, leap in the air at intervals, yell with exuberance. Laugh, even if you have to force it at first. Play a game of trying to make that forced laughter sound natural.

Sing gay ditties with all your might. Perform whimsical acts as they come to mind and do them as rapidly as possible without giving yourself time to think.

If you are in company tell jokes and encourage others to tell them to you. Practice your belly laugh, if a joke warrants it, and concentrate on making it sound as natural as possible.

Above all, do not stop to ask yourself, "Is it working? Am I less depressed that I was?"

Don't look back until you've managed to push yourself over to the bright side of the fence. You will know by the feel when you're there. Then you can afford to re-examine the problems that had seemed so insoluble before. You may even find yourself asking in surprise, "Why should I have been so depressed about **that?"**

RHYTHM TO DEFINE YOUR ROLE IN LIFE

Often your problem is not the need to physicalize any particular emotion but to adopt a more forceful overall rhythm that will enable us to play our role on the stage of life more convincingly.

Dr. Morehouse gives the following advice to anyone who wishes to change his personality.

"By deliberately accentuating your posture and the rhythms by which you move," Dr. Morehouse suggests, "you can almost trick your mind into believing you're a positive, dynamic person. A strange thing happens when you do this. Not only do you impress self-confidence upon your body, but other people begin to look on you as a person who has everything under control. And since we are all far more susceptible to our environments than we realize, we tend to pick up and accept the impressions others have of us."

YOUR TEMPO EXPRESSES YOU

Here's a bit of advice about your own tempo.

"Everybody goes through life in different tempos," wrote the genius Michael Chekhov. "It depends mainly on the temperament and the destiny of a person."

In others words, your tempo is one of the hallmarks of your individuality. So preserve it! Forget about keeping up with the Joneses materially, intellectually or socially. Live and develop within the framework of your own self. Which means **be yourself**. You will find it makes for a far better performance in the Play of Life.

TIMING

We now come to a word about timing. Correct timing is essential in performing our role in life. How many times, for instance, have you approached someone with an important idea or product, only to have it turned down brusquely?

Ask yourself if the trouble could have stemmed from bad timing? Even professional actors often become careless and misjudge their timing—with unhappy results.

One evening during personal appearances of **Bird Man of Alcatraz** Burt Lancaster found himself at Sardi's in New York, facing an audience of important people. Many were critical or downright hostile to Lancaster's sympathetic portrayal of the lifer, the late Robert Stroud.

Burt was in for a tough session of questions and answers. He knew it would help if he could break the feeling of tension in the room. So he rose to his feet and raised his arms in the characteristic gesture of Elmer Gantry, the role for which he had received an Oscar. His timing was perfect and he broke up his audience with laughter. The ensuing question and answer period was harmonious.

In Washington. D.C., Lancaster tried the same trick again. This time because of the success of the gesture in New York he carelessly performed it by rote. His timing was off. The gesture fell flat. Consequently the question and answer period was difficult.

AN IMPORTANT RULE

Don't ever take timing for granted! Before approaching anyone on an important matter, train yourself to ascertain if he is in a receptive mood. Should he happen to be troubled or preoccupied by some other problem, bide your time. Remember—impetuosity can very well result in failure.

ATMOSPHERE

So we come to atmosphere, which plays such an important part in all our undertakings. On stage it makes for a more vital portrayal. Therefore great care is taken to provide a setting that will not only catch the audience in its spell but also put the actors in the right mood. Music, sound effects landscape backdrops and lighting are employed for this purpose.

In films the establishment of atmosphere is considered so vital that credits are no longer introduced on a blank screen but against an "atmospheric" background appropriate to the movie. Music, color effects and geometric patterns, even the initial scenes of the movie itself, are used to establish atmosphere by the time the first line is spoken.

ATMOSPHERE ON THE STAGE OF LIFE

We, too, should take care to see that the setting is consonant with the scene if we want that scene to come off well. Most of us are already aware of this.

We realize the futility of discussing important business deals while riding a bus or attending a funeral or wedding or even during a chance encounter on a street. We try to arrange a more suitable setting for the occasion—a quiet luncheon in a good restaurant, a meeting in an office or even a home.

But though we may lay our physical settings with consummate care, we sometimes still come up with a loss. Why?

It is because atmosphere consists primarily, not of these physical settings, but of the moods of the persons found in them. If they are hostile or uncooperative the atmosphere will be a negative one.

ATMOSPHERES CAN BE CHANGED

It is not necessary, however, to resign oneself to a negative atmosphere, because atmospheres can be changed. In fact, this is always happening spontaneously in the world around us. We had a demonstration of it while visiting the Castle of Chillon in Vaud, Switzerland, at the east end of Lake Geneva.

Our visit happened to coincide with that of a troupe of schoolchildren. We came upon them in the somber courtroom where at one time alleged witches were tried. Now children were running gaily everywhere, chattering like blackbirds, swinging on the stout wooden posts where the unfortunate women had been bound. They were tracing with small lively fingers the deep scars in those posts made by the lash of the whips by which the women's confessions had been extracted.

While the children were there, the gloomy room, which had witnessed so much terror and suffering, was stripped of its tragic history. Instead, its stone walls resounded gaily to the happy present. After the children left, however, and silence fell again, the ancient atmosphere of grief, suffering and bigotry returned.

CHANGING A HOSTILE ATMOSPHERE

With a little effort you can change an unpleasant atmosphere. The next time you are confronted with hostility, don't retaliate with forceful language. You will never convince anyone that way. Remember the fable about the sun, the wind and the man in the overcoat?

Sun and Wind had a contest to see which one could make the man shed his coat. Wind had the first try. He blew fiercely, but the man only pulled his coat more tightly about him. Then Sun came out. Just a little of his pervasive warmth and the man quickly took off his coat.

Try Sun's trick, using the radiation methods you learned in Chapter 6, "Emotion." First radiate a positive atmosphere within yourself. Feel your body expanding and becoming buoyant with a joyous fluidic force that emanates from the center within you. Allow it to fill you and spread beyond you in a bright aura.

Then submerge the other person, hostile cloak and all, in that shining light. If your radiation has been strong and vital enough you will see the man shed his cloak and become amenable to what you have to say.

The authors have tried this little trick often with surprising effects. It works because it is a basic rule of the theater of Life that **the stronger atmosphere always wins.**

SOME METHODS USED BY OTHERS

On her personal appearance tours Elsa Lanchester breaks the ice between herself and her audiences with what the calls "the charm bracelet" approach. Elsa's charm bracelet consists of the thread of her life. On it she hangs a few interesting mementos. These are anecdotal souvenirs gathered from her many experiences. She relates them to the audience in a free and easy manner. Elsa told us there is nothing that breaks down barriers so easily as to make others your confidants in this way.

Dr. Tom Gaddis professor at Reed College in Portland, Oregon, and author of **Bird Man of Alcatraz,** told us he also uses this method to limber up a new class. He starts off by telling a little about himself and then encourages his students to do the same individually.

"This makes everyone familiar with everyone else and takes away inhibitions," he explained. "Because if you don't know who a person is you feel threatened by him and you tend to withdraw and throw up your reserves."

DICK VAN DYKE'S METHODS

Comedian Dick Van Dyke gave us these little tricks he uses to transform a dead-serious atmosphere into a more lively one.

First he appraises the situation which has brought on the atmosphere.

"Many people stop short with feeling the mood of situation," he said. "But few try to examine it and state the truth about it to themselves. The truth usually is that we're sitting there frozen stiff with fear, frantically trying to think of the right thing to say instead of just stating what we came to say in the first place. Once you realize this truth, the most serious situation assumes comic overtones. Play upon these overtones and you will be able to lighten the atmosphere."

Van Dyke also suggests the following little trick for lifting a gloomy mood among friends. It is based on the assumption that it takes the hair of the dog that bit you to affect a cure.

"If I find everyone down in the mouth I just go ahead and break into tears," he explained. "I sob and cry as realistically as possible.s This extreme awakens everyone to the ridiculousness of their pessimism and clears the atmosphere."

TWO EXERCISES

We conclude this chapter with two exercises. The first will show you how you can utilize off moments of the day to practice physicalizing emotions through bodily rhythms. The second will train you to become aware of the various atmospheres with which you are continually coming in contact.

These are valuable exercises because often even the most negative atmospheres are concealed under a surface of good will. Unless you learn to recongize and neutralize them first you will fail in putting across your projects.

EXERCISE 1 **An exercise suggested and followed by Lajos Egri, the famous playwright and teacher of dramatic writing**

You need to be walking to perform this exercise. A walk to work in the morning, that is an ideal time to do it.

As you stride along listen to the rhythm of yourself. Enjoy the pulse of life through muscles and blood, everything working in perfect coordination.

Experiment by humming tunes with different rhythms and moods and see how your body falls naturally into these rhythms.

If you watch your body as you might some personality not connected with you, you may rouse an admiration in yourself for perfect coordinations and responses. You will be glad and proud to make a friend of it, to allow it full leeway to express itself in the rhythms which it knows instinctively.

You will be surprised at how this exercise will relax your muscles and revitalize your brain for the hard work before you.

EXERCISE 2 **An exercise given by Michael Chekhov in his** To the Actor

Though atmosphere is intangible to the senses it is still very real psycologically. Alert your intuition to feel the various atmospheres which you may encounter during the course of the day. Try not to overlook or disregard atmospheres because they happen to be weak, subtle or carefully concealed from your sensory perceptions.

Pay especial attention to the fact that atmosphere does not confine itself to small segments of living. It is as universally present as the air we breathe is in the physical world. Become aware of it actually permeating the air, enveloping people and events, filling the rooms, floating through landscapes, pervading the life of which it is a part.

Watch people while they are surrounded by a certain atmosphere. Mark whether they move and speak in harmony, surrender to it, fight against it, to what extent they are sensitive or indifferent to it.

Finally, after a period of observation, when your ability to perceive different atmospheres is sufficiently trained and sharpened, begin to experiment with yourself. Consciously and deliberately try to submit to certain atmospheres, "listening" to them as you listen to music, and let them influence you.

Let them call up within you your own individual feelings. Begin to move and speak in harmony with the different atmosphere you encounter. Then choose cases where you can oppose a specific atmosphere. Do battle with it simply for the fun of seeing it transform itself into something you have willed.

Once you have acquired skill in changing atmospheres you will find yourself in possession of a valuable tool to enable you to play your life role more effectively than you ever imagined possible.

nine

The Art of Human Understanding

YOUR FELLOW PLAYERS

NO MATTER how polished your performance in the play of life, it will fall flat unless your fellow players are taken into account. Life is made up not only of action, but of reaction. Therefore, unless you interest yourself in the psychology of those you wish to influence you will never succeed in getting to them.

Lawyers find it pays to study the character and biography of the judge who will be trying their case. Good teachers acquaint themselves with the backgrounds of their pupils to keep from classifying as juvenile delinquency what is merely a typical sociological attitude.

Successful restaurateurs realize customers are as interested in personal attention as in the food. Much of the popularity of the Kowloon Restaurant in Los Angeles, for instance, is due to the traditional Chinese hospitality that its owners, George Lim and Joe Ho, show every guest. Usually such hospitality is to be found only in the privacy of Chinese homes; but Lim and Ho recognized its value in their business enterprise.

Many commercial firms rely on the personal touch to hold their customers. There asre a number of sumptuous banks in Los

Angeles. But we know of a homey little branch bank which keeps most of its patrons because of the interested approach of its clerks.

"Our customers are as personal to us as members of our own family." a teller told us. "What happens to them touches us all. We feel our responsibility toward them goes deeper than just looking after their money. We even provide a kind of confessional for those who need to unload their private troubles."

If you are in a business which brings you into daily contact with the public you might take a lesson from these tellers. Try to meet the needs of each one—as an individual. You will find that it not only makes your work less humdrum but that it also brings monetary rewards, for people like being noticed and will come back again and again.

THE INTUITION OF A SALESMAN

A salesman must train himself to understand the individual psychology of his prospective customers. He must be adept at following their thought processes and even at guiding them until he has roused the enthusiasm necessary to make his sale.

Whenever he tackles a group, the shrewd salesmen can sense at once the skeptical ones, even though they make no outward display of their feeling. He makes a special effort to win them over—and knows when he is succeeding. This is why people credit a good salesman with intuition.

HOW IS YOUR INTUITION WORKING?

Intuition is not a magical hunch that comes out of the blue. You can train your intuition by watching for the behavior patterns of people, just as the good salesman does.

Practice your observation and attention exercises with particular emphasis on others' behavior patterns. When you have noticed a number of such patterns, classify them. You will see that nine times out of ten the different people who display the same pattern will share the same psychological foundation.

Take the man who talks glibly and convincingly but never looks you in the eye. Your intuition warns you to be wary of him. Similarly you will know that the man who has surface calm is suffering from inner disquiet if he is smoking cigarettes chain fashion.

One word of caution is necessary, however. Be sure to submit every intuitive hunch to your rational mind for careful analysis. Some hunches are based on physical characteristics instead of on behavior patterns. If you are distrustful of a person because of the shape of his nose or the color of his eyes, for instance, dismiss that hunch as useless. It came perhaps from an unpleasant childhood experience with a person who possessed a similar feature.

Intuitional alertness to behavior patterns can help you decide which people to trust and which to beware of. It will also save you from being taken by slick operators.

If your goal is to achieve something worthwhile, intuition can be your first step forward. The next is to establish rapport with the person whose help you need. With some people this rapport is easily effected at the very first approach. But you will find that with others, for one reason or another, you are unable to rouse the warm outgoing emotion in yourself which is so vital to your success.

THE USE OF SPECIFIES

What should you do when you meet a person with whom you cannot establish rapport? Here is a method Estelle Harman gives her drama students and which many actors and actresses use to help arouse the emostion they require. Miss Harman calls it the use of specifies.

It begins with a simple phrase, "I...... him **because** ...." The player inserts the name of the emotion he wishes to arouse—love, hate, suspicion, dislike, etc.- after the "I." But since you have no need to call on these varied emotions, your particular phrase should run, **"I like** him **because** ...." The magic word is "because."

When you are confronted with a person who makes you start freezing, repeat this simple phrase to yourself. Then look him over carefully until you find one thing about him that you can wholeheartedly **like.** Don't try to look for something profound. That small item needn't be more than the cut of his suit or the shape of his ears.

Once you have found a point of contact you can complete your phrase, as, for instance, "I like him **because** his teeth are so even and white." Now address all your remarks directly to that likeable characteristic.

If you feel genuine approval of it the magic "because" **must** work for you. What happens is this: when you concentrate on that one positive quality the other person, without knowing what you are approving of, senses your approval all the same. He begins to react warmly toward you.

It is as though he has unconsciously picked up your magic "because and is flashing it back to you in this form, "I like you **because** I feel you like me." No frosty atmosphere can continue under these circumstances.

DEEPER RELATIONSHIPS

Sometimes, however, the act of human understanding requires more than this surface rapport. This is especially true in the intimacy of family life, where a number of unique and sometimes apparently incompatible personalities are thrown together and required to get along in this play of life. It's evident that frictions will arise. But it is equally true that these frictions can be eliminated if it is possible to get into the other person's skin and see things from his viewpoint.

Actors must do this if they want their characters to come alive on the stage. Therefore they go to great lengths to insure understanding of the people they portray.

Karl Malden makes copious notes about the history, background and characteristics of the character he is to play. He discards the first set of notes and makes a second. He repeats this process until he begins to get the "feel" of the man.

"One day when I was studying a role in this manner, "he told an acting seminar, "I suddenly found myself out in the garden working. Since I hadn't worked in a garden for two years I couldn't understand it, until I realized I was there because I'd decided my character was a man who would end up in the garden. Then I knew I was getting myself into his shoes at last."

PSYCHODRAMA

Many of us for the sake of harmony would be willing, like Karl Malden, to work at "understanding" the other fellow. For people like us, psychologists have discovered a form of acting which enables us to put ourselves in the other fellow's shoes.

It is called psychodrama.

The father of psychodrama is Dr. Jacob L. Moreno, the former Viennese who is now an American citizen. To explore this modern development of psychology, we visited the home of Dr. Robert Bartlett Haas, head of the department of Arts and Humanities for the Extension Division of the University of Southern California at Los Angeles. He had been personally taught by Dr. Moreno.

Dr. Haas told us that psychodrama, under a trained therapist, his been used to aid people with deep-seated neuroses. Educators have also used it to train children to meet the challenges of life.

In psychodrama children are encouraged to act out true-life plays, usually centered on some unpleasant situation that they have experienced. The child who suffered the experience plays the lead role. Other children are assigned the supporting parts. The experience is acted out according to the child's directions.

This is followed by a repetition of the play with a reversal of roles. The child now takes the part of the person who he feels has mistreated him. Usually it is the parent or teacher or another adult in authority.

This technique of reversing roles enables the child to get a better understanding of the situation and of the other person's side of the picture.

Dr. Haas told us the story of a young mother who successfully played a little psychodrama with her seven-year-old daughter in their home. The mother wanted to cure the child of the annoying habit of constantly interrupting her whenever the mother sat down to the piano.

One night mother and child agreed to an exchange of roles. The child played the part of "mother" with enthusiastic realism. The time came for her, in the role of her mother, to sit down to the piano. Immediately the mother as "child" hovered nearby, interrupting her constantly.

Suddenly the little girl dropped her role of "mother" to say earnestly, "Oh, mother, how you must hate having me interrupt your playing the way I always do. I never realized until now how annoying it must be."

Thus the mother had got the idea across without a harsh reprimand that would have alienated the child.

Psychodrama, according to Dr. Haas, is useful in helping to solve conflicts in the home, especially between children and adults, when these conflicts are not the result of deep-seated neuroses requiring trained therapists. In fact, he told us, he receives enthusiastic reports from teenagers who have studied psychodrama under him and who have practiced it to iron out problems with their parents or other family members.

If there are conflicts in your home, perhaps a little psychodrama will solve them. Try changing roles with a member of your family and looking at life, and especially at yourself, through the eyes of the other person. Meanwhile he will be playing your role and perhaps getting some insights for himself.

TWO IMPORTANT RULES

There are two important rules that must be followed if psychodrama is to be used successfully.

1. Never play psychodrama with the thought of "showing up" the other person. You must be sincere in wanting to find the truth about yourself.

2. Every act and line of this impromptu drama must be exactly that—impromptu, and therefore completely spontaneous. Otherwise you won't get a true picture of life. Remember, this isn't creative art. It's a remedy and its sole purpose is to achieve a harmonious solution to a conflict

WHEN YOU CAN'T USE PSYCHODRAMA

In many cases, psychodrama may be impractical. If so, here is another method to resolve a lack of rapport between you and another.

First, make a careful list of your relations with this person during the preceding day. Ask yourself how many times you offered your services to him in little ways. How many compliments did you pay him? How many pleasant things did you say or do for him?

Think back to the negative things you may have done to offend this person, either intentionally or unintentionally. When you addressed him, was your voice pleasant and cheerful or did it carry the querulousness of past irritations? Did you wear a chip-on-the-shoulder attitude and take umbrage at remarks that weren't meant to be unfriendly? Were you actually **looking** for slights?

When you have completed this list, plan your course of action to put an end to the conflict. Begin by determining to reform yourself in one small way at first. You will find it often takes little effort to end a state of disharmony that may have been years in the making.

ONE COMPLIMENT A DAY

Zina Provendie tells of a woman who came to her complaining that for the past ten years her husband had completely ignored her. She was, the women said, ready for a divorce.

"Try a little drama for a month on your husband before you sue for that divorce," Zina suggested. "Give him at least one sincere compliment a day, even if it's only on the tie he's wearing."

The woman agreed to try it.

A few weeks later she phoned Miss Provendie in great excitement.

"I have a date with my husband downtown for luncheon," she said jubilantly. "It's the first time in our married life he's done such a thing. Our romance is starting all over again."

What one compliment a day did to help this woman create a more effective role in relation to another member of her family can, perhaps, be repeated in your case. Try it and see.

HOW ABOUT YOUR CHILDREN?

It may be that the judicious use of compliments will dispel sudden streaks of contrariness or defiance in your children. Often such behavior problems spring from lack of recognition of the child's role in the family drama. Ask yourself frankly what part your children play in your life.

Are they just responsibilities to be fed and clothed and sent to school? Do you feel you solve all their problems by paying fat premiums on the insurance policy that will take care of their physical needs should anything happen to you?

Why not try paying similar dividents to secure their emotional future? It takes so little, really, to make a child feel he has a vital role in your life.

"In my opinion the best gift a child can have is the gift of emotional security and happiness within," Celeste Holm told us. "When he is in possession of this treasure he can afford to be generous with other people in his adulthood."

JAMES STEWART AND THE TANNER BUS DRIVERS

Generosity is such a vital part of living your role fully that your concern for other should not stop at home.

James Stewart is a long-time star whose name and fortune are both made. He is in the enviable position of being able to run his life as he pleases. Yet Jimmy is never above taking time out to perform a thoughtful act if it will help someone else.

Take the Tanner bus driver who route tourists past his big house on North Roxbury Drive in Beverly Hills.

Jimmy knows it's bread and butter for these men, so he goes out of his way to stage a little scene now and then to make their customers feel they're getting their money's worth. He not only strolls about outside where he can be seen but greets the bus drivers by name and goes over to chat briefly with them.

You'll find similar actions, insignificant in themselves, with which you can brighten someone's day or help him in his work. If you make a point of doing something like this each day, even if it is no more than a cheery greeting or a word of approval, you will find your own role in life enriched. For there is nothing more therapeutic to body and mind than giving for its own sake.

SPECIALIZED UNDERSTANDING

Sometimes a profession requires its members to develop an even deeper understanding of others to fulfil their role properly. One of these is the practice of medicine. The doctor has not only to realize the psychological needs of his patients, but he must also be ready to fortify them in moments of crisis.

Often a doctor is faced with a agonizing task of breaking the diagnosis of mortal illness to a patient and his family. He must use comfort and understanding. Dr. Rex Kennamer will always remember the day he faced Gary Cooper and told the actor gently that he was dying of cancer.

"I had to put myself in his shoes so that I would say, the right thing to him," Dr. Kennamer told us. "I had to tell him the facts with comfort and at the same time give him a minor ray of hope, for no one should be plunged into utter despair. Yet I also had to let him know there probably wasn't any hope.

But Gary Cooper was a real trouper. During his long career he had put himself too often into the shoes of other people not to realize the anguish Dr. Kennamer, his long-time friend and doctor, was suffering. Early the next morning the doctor received a phone call.

"Doc," Coop's cheerful voice came over the wire. "I know that was a terrible thing we put you through yesterday, but I want you to know you did the right thing."

LOVE WORKS WONDERS

Perhaps you aren't a doctor. And perhaps you're not in a position to give comfort to a conscientious doctor who has had to confront you with bad news. But there do come times to you, when a few words of understanding, a small but sincere expression of love, can spell the difference between life and death for another.

"I found out what a great healer love is when I was in the hospital recuperating from my heart attack," Lee J. Cobb told us. "When the girl I later married first started visiting me I was very low and depressed. It was she who woke the will to live in me. All the doctors and nurses at the hospital noticed the change in my spirits at once."

Love has the power not only to cure the sick one but also to vitalize you, the giver.

Dr. Norman Vincent Peale, who is known for his dynamic sermons, told us that when he began his career he suffered from such excruciating shyness that it was difficult for him to face the public. Some good advice from the late Harry Davenport came to his rescue, and its has stood him in good stead through the years.

"I never address an audience without first projecting my love to them as Harry taught me to do," he explained. "It is the only way I know to conquer the fear I still would feel if I did not do so."

Try projecting love when you are faced with a difficult or frightening relationship with your fellowmen. It should almost miraculously, smooth the way for you.

KEEP YOUR ANTENNA UP

Don't hold back your love until you are directly faced with situations that call for it in a conspicuous way. Keep your antenna up at all times. They may be people in your immediate vicinity who have real need for it.

Usually our neighbors' lives seem so matter-of-fact that it never occurs to us they may be having deep trouble handling their roles and are craving a little understanding or word of comfort. We are apt to believe that tragedy happens only to distant individuals facing great crises.

But thoughtful Dolores Hart once told us, "People with real troubles aren't necessarily the ones who live across town from you. A fine young man next door to me in my neighborhood killed himself. If he'd had someone to talk things over with it might have been different."

Keep your antenna up for such people. They are worth your trouble. For you will discover any energy that you center constructively on helping others will come back to you in a deeper fulfillment of your own life role.

HELPING ANOTHER PERSON TRANSFORM HIS LIFE ROLE

In an earlier chapter we explained how, through the use of your imagination, you could change your own role in life to a more effective one. Do you realize that imagination is such a powerful force that you can also employ it to help another revitalize his life role?

Here is how a Los Angeles policeman named Mickey Finn changed the role of a whole group of young boys trapped in the slums of Los Angeles. Mickey's first beat was on North Broadway, a tough section of town. He was supposed to ride herd on the juvenile delinquents who hung out there.

But Mickey don't see them as delinquents. His imagination pictured them as good kids in need of guidance. He decided what they needed was a club house to keep them off the streets. He dug into his own pocket to provide it for them.

He established it in a rundown building. He hocked his station wagon, he borrowed on his salary, and often went without food to keep the club house going for his "good" boys. No sacrifice was too great for him.

Mickey, who told us the story of his work with the boys, described the following incident to demonstrate how his faith in them was amply rewarded. One night while he was lying ill in his small apartment, thinking of how good a big steak would taste, there was a knock at his door. He opened it. Two of his club members came in, with a picnic basket filled with fried chicken and all that goes with it.

Mickey stared at the basket. All he could think of was that both these boys had already been in trouble with the law for breaking into shops.

Then one of those boys broke the silence.

"You don't need to worry, Mickey," he said. "We **earned** the money at the bell park selling soda pop."

Mickey had imagined "good boys" where others had seen only "juvenile delinquents." His boys had responded by living up to that image.

TRY IT YOURSELF

Is there someone you would like to help play a more effective role in life? Then sit down and paint a picture of him as he would actually be if he were, in your opinion, constructively fulfilling himself.

Dwell on that picture; be sure to infuse it with the warmth of your feeling. Then, whenever you come in contact with this individual, put your image between yourself and him. Treat him as if he **were** that image in actuality.

If your imagination is strong and vital you will see results quickly; as a matter of fact, you will see results eventually even with the use of a little imagination. People, like plants, animals and all living things in nature, respond without fail to the warmth of human approval and good wishes.

NOW FOR THE SCARS OF THE PAST

As you perfect the art of human understanding, you will find courage to tackle more difficult jobs. Go back in memory to the former friend who once did something so despicable that you've never been able to forgive him.

Forget what was done; concentrate instead on the person who did it. Try to see the situation from his viewpoint. Perhaps terrific pressures forced him into the act of wronging you. Reexamine his psychological background. Is it made up of a long history of humiliations, rejections and loneliness that molded him from his childhood into the negative role he is playing today?

If you bring true compassion to your study, a marvelous thing will begin to happen to you. The old hate will disappear, lifting its burden from your life. For hate is a crushing depressant and no one who harbors it can play his role effectively.

Perhaps as you go over the circumstances impartially, you may discover you were really at fault; that it was false assumptions on your part and not treachery on your friend's that really led to the rift.

From time to time we all commit these errors in passing judgment on our fellow men. Why?

LETTING YOUR HIGHER SELF BE THE JUDGE

Michael Chekhov, in his **To the Director and Playwright**, edited posthumously by Charles Leonard, suggests that because we allow the personal ego to stand at the helm of our lives, we make great mistakes in judging other people. This ego skims over life, glibly giving out criticisms, freely voicing condemnations, passing judgments that are often influenced by secret jealousies.

Yet, as Chekhov points out, there is a higher self in every one of us. It keeps itself hidden, does not obtrude or force its opinions and wisdom on the ego. But it **will** answer if we make a habit of asking it to do our judging for us.

Try to let the self voice its compassionate opinion of all human beings who are in the cast of your play of life. You will gain much from such an open-minded attitude.

"If you enter into people's lives with sympathy and understanding you will acquire more charm than you can get from all the instructions given in the best charm schools in the country," Zina Provendie, our charm expert, promises.

Communion with one's fellow men does not involve a static set of rules. It is a vital force whose invisible currents radiate from us and magnetize the air around us.

"The more we indulge and lavish it [love], the more it can give us in return, "Michael Chekhov goes on. "I have actually seen this at work in myself and in many of my colleagues."

Try it out to discover how miraculously his expansive attitude can magnetize your role in life.

TWO EXERCISES

We are concluding this chapter with two exercises that may amuse and help you take the first steps toward putting yourself in the other fellow's shoes.

EXERCISE 1 **An exercise by Bob Gist**

Choose some person—anyone with whom you have come in contact during the day. Put yourself completely in his shoes; get the feel of life from his vantage point.

Let us say you choose to play a butler. It is not enough to walk around in the dignified impassivity which type butlers portray on the screen. Ask yourself questions?

Why did I decide on this profession? What is my mother like? Where did I go to school? What do I do when I'm not butling? Do I have a girl?

Build up a flesh-and-blood life as a butler until you actually become this man.

The exercise will demonstrate that there are many interesting and secret facets in the makeup of each person. The next time you come face to face with a maitre d'hotel or a butler or bellboy, you will see him with new eyes. He will be not just a fixture for your convenience, but a human being playing an important role in life.

EXERCISE 2 **Suggested by Michael Chekhov**

Choose any person. It does not matter, whether you know him or not. In privacy, set your face the way his face is set. Practice his mannerisms. Do not look in the mirror, however, to check on yourself. By the feel you will know when you approximate his expression. If he has a physical deformity approximate this, also.

You will be surprised at the subtle changes that come over your personality as you get the feel of him. You will also be concentrating on the clues which will help you establish typical behavior patterns and the psychological characteristics that go with them.

ten

Yourself

LET'S TALK ABOUT YOU

NOW we come to the most important subject of all—yourself.

WHAT DO YOU THINK OF YOURSELF?

Perhaps you haven't really given yourself genuine thought. Or perhaps you have been looking at yourself in a deprecatory manner. We are apt to feel guilty thinking about ourselves. And when we do think about ourselves we tend to accept the image the world throws back at us.

In this way we lose the depth of individuality that would make our role in life such an exciting and worthwhile adventure. To remedy such a state of affairs, this chapter will deal with you specifically, offering suggestions to bring out the truly great actor that lives within you.

YOU AND YOUR INFERIORITY COMPLEX

Perhaps you feel there's no hope for you. Your inferiority complex is so bad that you couldn't change if you tried. So we use this excuse for explaining our failures and our fears—in short, our background acting!

However, an inferiority complex is the most normal thing in the world. This is because it's based on actuality. We are all really inferior, in some degree, to every other person in the world.

Take your looks, for instance! Do you secretly feel that with a more attractive front the world would be yours? Has it ever occurred to you that some people have inferiority complexes just because of their good looks?

It look Jeff Hunter a long while to reach the point where he'd accept leading roles. He had been in the habit of choosing supporting parts. He was afraid that people hired him for his looks and that he'd let them down when he started to act.

Many of the screen's glamor girls have such inferiority complexes about their acting abilities that they place an inordinate emphasis on appearance to carry them through. One of the screen's most beautiful actresses, Gina Lollobrigida, was so terrified of destroying her image as an irresistible siren that she insisted on wearing glamorous makeup even in the role of a street gamin.

In contrast, Sophia Loren found early in her career that looks have little to do with playing a role effectively. She learned to appear homely whenever the part called for it. Such a role, that of Cesira in **Two Women,** won Sophia her Academy Award as the best actress of 1964.

THE SELF IS SUPERIOR

All outstanding actors and actresses come to the final realization that great acting springs from the revelation of the intrinsic self. They know that in that self lies their claim to genuine superiority, for being unique, it cannot be duplicated. No matter how inadequately these people may handle their private lives, the real self they display in their professional work guarantees an outstanding performance.

To prove that the commanding presence of a screen personality is due solely to exposing the unique self to the public eye, the late actress Carole Lombard liked to play this trick. She would go down a crowded city street acting like a simple member of the crowd around her. No one would take the least notice. Then all at once she would "transform" herself into Carole Lombard and be almost instantly recognized.

Recently Rock Hudson rented a car and drove through the Deep South from Miami to Atlanta. His only disguise was a pair of hornrimmed glasses, which he actually wears in off-screen life. He mixed freely with people. Yet despite his arresting figure and familiar face he was recognized less than ten times during that long drive.

Because he wanted anonymity he had deliberately retreated into background acting to give himself this change of pace.

PUT FORWARD A BETTER SELF

Perhaps you may feel this is all well for film and stage personalities who are born with latent magnetic personalities. You yourself are so dull that nothing possibly can help.

Then you'll be interested in the story Tony Barr told us of the young poultry expert who called himself a chicken doctor. He had come to Hollywood from the Midwest on a vacation and for the fun of it registered for one of Barr's beginners courses for aspiring actors. He was an awkward, self-conscious fellow, so tonguetied he could scarcely get out two words in sequence. Barr didn't think the fellow would find the courage to continue those classes, where he would have to put himself on public display.

But the young man did and finally his self broke through. From then on he had a lark. By the time he was ready to go back home he had become a self-assured out-going person with a new zest for living.

"This acting is a piece of cake," he told Barr. "It's changed my whole life."

You can change your personality, just as he did, by putting in some effort. So why not take the first step:

RECOGNIZE YOUR MASK

Sit down alone; with your magic projection machine throw onto your imaginary screen the image of yourself as you have been presenting it to the world.

What do you see there? A failure? A mere cog in a machine? A person without individuality or character—just one more cipher in a multitude of ciphers? A forlorn, ugly, rejected human being?

If this is what you see, it means you are on the outside looking in. All you see is the mask you present to the world, which you have come to accept as the real you. It is no more the real you than the clothes you wear.

Unfortunately, we construct these ugly masks out of a conglomeration of minor events stretching back over the years. And we even accept them without question from the hands of others.

THE MASK OF REJECTION

Bob Gist told us of one of his students whose beautiful spirit was crammed behind the dull mask she had accepted as her own personality when her husband deserted her.

"I'm not only ugly. I'm the ugliest person alive," her mask mourned for the whole world to hear.

But the girl was sincere about wanting to be an actress. She came to classes regularly. She conscientiously performed the dramatic exercises. These included improvisations and dramatic renditions of situations in which she was theoretically placed by her teacher.

At first she reacted only to the promptings of the mask and consequently her acting was wooden and unconvincing. But she was encouraged to search below her mask and call up organic responses from her inner self.

The girl cooperated fully. Conquering her apathy she reached down into her real self for material for her portrayals. As she came into closer contact with that self, her acting became more vibrant. But of greater importance was the complete change in her everyday personality.

She began to dress smartly. She started wearing lipstick again. Her sullen mask-like face began to glow with a natural radiance. Presently no one would have recognized the beautiful young woman as the ugly duckling who had first come to study with Gist.

THE MASK OF IMPORTANCE

Perhaps, on the other hand, you're wearing a mask of "importance." This mask insists on going after every material possession Mr. Jones owns simply for the sake of keeping up.

"We spend our lives accumulating status symbols for only one reason, Jack Lemmon told us, "approval and the applause it brings. What we should realize is that applause means something only when we earn it by being more truly ourselves instead of trying to please and impress everyone."

YOU ARE NOT YOUR MASK

Once you have taken a good look at the image presented to the world, tell yourself firmly that it is not the real you. The real you does not feel rejected because somebody deserts it, or insecure without carloads of material possessions. It does not accept a few failings as an indication of failure, nor will it tolerate being relegated to the role of background actor. It will fight back with conflict.

The real you is a great and wonderful being in which all the creative forces of nature and spirit have combined to fashion something wholly unique. 'There is no one like you in the whole world. There no one in the whole world who can play your role as you yourself can play it, for you were created to that end.

As James Cagney used to say to the extras who worked with him, "My railroad may be longer than yours, but yours is just as wide."

So whether you think your role is big or small, don't underestimate its importance. Remember: It's up to you to make it important.

GETTING DOWN TO PARTICULARS

As a first step make a list of the qualities, not earthly possessions, you would display as a new personality. We all possess fine qualities because they are part of the heritage of the human race. In some people they are scarcely developed; in others they are repressed. But with effort we can all waken them in ourselves.

HOW GEORGE HAMILTON DID IT

After you list your qualities, select the one most important to you and begin to work on it. Once you see results, you will be eager to experiment with other qualities.

Here are techniques used by actors to bring out the qualities they needed to portray a character adequately.

George Hamilton is a sophisticated, intellectual young modern. He had to transform himself into the ingenouas Fabrizio, the Italian boy in **Light in the Piazza,** before he could attempt the role. Following Zina Provendie's advice he forgot his usual self. Instead, he filled his mind with the love, warmth and generosity that were attributes of the Italian boy. He made them shine in his eyes and he demonstrate them in his gestures.

As a result George played to perfection a role that was diametrically opposed to the personality people associated with him.

You yourself can **think** into being the qualities you want if you concentrate on them wholeheartedly enough. Practice radiating them in the color which expresses the quality most vitally to you. Walk in its rhythm. Relax and let this rhythm take complete possession of you.

SUPPOSE YOU STILL CAN'T GET INT0 THE FEEL

If you still can't get into the feel of the quality take out your easel and paint a picture to express it. Even though you are no artist, the effort you make to put this special quality into pictorial form will help to rouse it

Or try singing it Singing is a great medium for releasing hidden qualities and bringing the self to the force.

Any kind of music is great therapy.

Dean Martin told us that when he first arrived in Hollywood he was so shy he used to sit mute and miserable in a corner. He came from a background of gambling casinos and night clubs, and his way of talking murdered the English language. Because he was so handsome, his aloofness was misinterpreted as snobbishness.

Dean decided to **sing** his way into self-confidence. He began to sing at gatherings where previously he had been too tongue-tied to open his mouth. He made a pleasing impression on other which increased self-confidence. Today Dean is one of the screen's most self-assured actors.

Perhaps you haven't enough voice to expose in public. But if you like to sing, try it, anyway-at home, in the shower. Let yourself go! Choose the melodies that express qualities you are trying to develop. The warm vital emotion which singing rouses brings these feelings to the surface. Then you can capture them to carry with you through the day.

THE MAGIC "AS IF"

The magic "as if" is another method many actors and actresses use to vitalize the qualities they need for their roles. It was devised by Stanislavski for his pupils. Here is how it works.

When Jeff Corey wanted to create the personality of the wino in **Lady in a Cage** he behaved **as if** he were afraid of all art objects and shied away from them. Only Corey knew what his character feared. The audience was only aware of the eccentric arrhythmic patterns of the charater he was playing. But those erratic movements conveyed more vividly than words the impression of insanity.

Similarly, the late Roman Bohnen, in the memorable part of Candy in **Of Mice and Men**, acted as if he were behind a plaster wall with one eye set against a chink, watching the world but never participating in it. Again, though the audience had no knowledge of the image in Bohnen's mind, they were deeply stirred by the poignant little man he created.

We play this magic "as if' game all the time without being aware of it. Unfortunately, too often we select negative "as it" formulas to reflect to the world. Then we can t understand why we're the victims of ill will.

If you have unconsciously projected a negative "as if'' picture, deliberately change it to a positive "as if" and you will discover how quickly the attitude of others toward you follows suit.

Here are some brief trial exercises by which you can familiarize yourself with the formula. You may think of other exercises yourself.

Try walking **as if** on cloud nine. Or start behaving **as if** you're a king wearing a golden crown, or a beautiful woman who has the world at your feet.

Of course, People won't see the image you are evoking, but you'll be amazed at how quickly they pick up the quality which it represents.

WHEN THE MAGIC "AS IF" WON'T WORK

There may be moments when you find some desired quality so alien to your conscious mind that even with a magic "as if" you cannot call it into being. If so, solve the problem by putting your powers of observation to work.

Select a person in whom you recognize the quality you wish for yourself. Check his gestures, his mannerisms, his tone of voice, his body stance. Then start aping him—in private at first-but with feeling. Throw yourself wholeheartedly into the role.

At first you will depend almost entirely on the gestures and mannerisms of the person you are copying, Then gradually, as you step into his shoes, you will get the **feeling** which animates him. Once his happens, you can begin to express it in your own way.

Use of his methods should be only the booster that sends your space ship into orbit. To be effective you **must** develop your own style.

A WAY FOR EVERYONE

You have a particular style, just as everyone on stage, screen. and television has. To ignore that style is to "step out of character" and a poor performance will invariably result.

Compare the acting style of Richard Boone and the late Gary Cooper. Boone has an earthly forthright manner. Cooper had a more easygoing, quite quality. Yet both styles are symbols of manliness.

If you're the quiet type like "big Coop," you needn't throw your weight around to get your due. It won't impress anyone, because your rhythm will be wrong. There are other effective ways of getting what you want Cooper knew them all-and used them, off stage well as on.

Once on location he found his dressing room at an inconvenient distance from the camera. Instead of creating a scene he just grinned pleasantly and began ambling back and forth between the set and his room to get various things he "needed." He wasted a great deal of everyone's time that first day with his good-natured ambling.

The following day, without a comment from anyone, he found his dressing room moved closer to the camera.

Use your imagination to solve your problems in your own style. You'll be far more effective and what's more, you won't end the day with a headache caused by the tensions of playing your part out of character.

MAYBE YOU'RE AN EXTROVERT

If you are an extrovert don't feel obliged to conceal your expansiveness under a false cloak of modesty. Don't be afraid to take your bows openly.

Writer Walter Reisch told us how one great actor who craved attention solved his problem. He was the late Emil Jannings, who had spent most of his life on the European stage and was accustomed to many nightly curtain calls.

In Hollywood he missed those bows. So whenever there was a touring company in town he went to the theater to look up some actor friend in the troupe. He always managed to arrive backstage about 10:45.

Shortly after his arrival the curtain would come down and the actors would go out for their bows. Jannings, unnoticed, would join the cast and take a bow with them. In this whimsical and harmless way he was able to satisfy his need for attention.

Even those who recognized Jannings never resented his presence. As a great artist he had earned the right to all the bows and applause he could get. Remember. You have as much right as Jannings to take bows if you have earned them. Accept the praise with genuine and outgoing pleasure. It's as much yours as the suit or dress you're wearing.

Jackie Gleason put it to us this way, "You see a person in a large organization who proudly displays a watch or some other memento he has received from the boss in appreciation of his outstanding performance. The talent you possess, for every one of us possesses a talent of some sort, is a similar gift of appreciation from your Creator. Surely, then, you will gladly and proudly show it off."

ARE YOU SEEKING APPLAUSE?

Many people think applause is due only for the big accomplishments of the business, political, artistic or social worlds. And they engage in a cut-throat competition for the sole sake of being important. The person who seeks applause for this sort of surface deed will never be satisfied.

The only way to bring applause that is truly satisfy is to play our role in its richest capacity.

Many actors and actresses realize the need to express themselves in ways beyond their acting. This is a side of Hollywood that has never really been explored. In the field of painting alone there are many notable artist among film personalities–Kim Novak, Claudette Colbert, Red Skelton, Edward G. Robinson, Richard Whorf, Hedy Lamarr and Richard Conte, to name just a few.

Jack Lemmon plays the piano and composes music in his spare time. Bob Mitchum writes poetry, Yvette Mimieux short stories. William Holden, Yul Brynner and Dame Flora Robson study languages.

The list of avocations among stars is almost endless. Vincent Price has made practically a full-time career for himself lecturing on art, and he is considered an authority. Mickey Rooney always had a desire to teach, particularly in the performing arts, and the desire led him finally to set up a national chain of schools called Mickey Rooney's Actor's Workshops. He told us his next move will be the founding of The University of Imagination, which will embrace all the arts.

YOU, TOO, CAN CREATE

Lajos Egri points out that we are equipped with several talents which should be developed not for the sake of monetary gain but for the sheer pleasure of creativity.

So ask yourself if there's something you've always wanted to do but have lacked the courage to start. Perhaps painting, writing, gardening, decorating, or something so far out there's not a name for it. Cultivate it! Attend classes where you'll meet others interested in the same subject.

Don't concern yourself about the world's reaction. Work for the sheer joy of it.Perhaps you will turn out to be another Grandma Moses and your paintings will bring you fame. And you may discover then that all the acclaim in the world can't equal the pleasure of creating something for its own sake.

THE SOCIAL SERVICES

Perhaps instead of creative work your interest lies in helping others. This kind of service is therapeutic for physical and mental ailments. Dr.Rex Kennamer recommends it to his patients who suffer from a common ailment--loneliness. He advises interest in church or political work, or in volunteer service at hospitals, orphanages or schools for the handicapped.

There are many worthy causes that will repay your efforts with a sense of fulfilment and completion. Just make sure that you look for your reward in the doing and not in expectation of gratitude.

THE REWARDS

As you express your creativity, you will discover how vitally you are enlarging your role in life. Soon, old hesitancics will disappear. New self-confidence will take their place, How the world treats you will no longer carry such traumatic weight. You will no longer feel slighted at apparent snubs and barbs.

Dudley Murphy, former film director and present owner of the famous Holiday House near the Malibu film colony on the Pacific Coast Highway in California, told us he can pick out the truly important people among his patrons.

"The people who have not yet found themselves and are uncertain of their roles in life," explained Mr. Murphy, "have to assume pompous airs to convince themselves and others they've somebodies. They're the ones who are always deeply hurt when they're not recognized immediately, even though it's only the second time they've been to the restaurant."

In constrast Mr. Murphy likes to remember the man who came in one night with an easy smile, extended his hand and said cheerfully. "Good evening, Mr. Murphy."

"I'd known him for twenty years," Mr. Murphy told us, "but I hadn't seen him for four and I couldn't for the life of me recall him."

The man noticed Mr. Murphy's quizzical look and his smile broadened.

"Cary Grant, sir," he introduced himself.

Cary Grant's ego could afford to go unrecognized because he'd come to recognize his own self. It's an axiom that you **have** to recognize and **have** respect for your self before you can show tolerance for the foibles of others.

" Self-love is not the same thing as selfishness," Dick Van Dyke told us when we pressed him for an analysis of the secret magnetism of his brand of humor. " Self-love is true regard for your self. And the person who possesses this virtue is able to laugh at the world's barbs and even at his own pomposity when it gets the better of him."

THE VALUE OF LAUGHTER

Once you have reached the point of laughing at your mistakes yon have brought your true self into focus with the world.

Drama coaches realize the efficacy of self-laughter as a cure for self-conciousness in their beginner students. When Diane Baker, who today is a self-assured young actress, first arrived at Warner Brothers to study under Estelle Harman, she was a very self-conscisous young girl. She walked with her head down, spoke in a quiet voice and couldn't get on stage without clinging to furniture.

Miss Harman knew Diane would never make a good actress as long as she was so desperately concerned about her appearance. So she gave Diane clown assignments. When the actress realized she was going to look silly no matter how she performed those assignments, she loosened up. Thus she learned that poise is not a matter of outer appearance but of vitality of the inner self.

YOU DON'T HAVE TO BE A CLOWN

You don't have to wear a clown costume or a mask to make use of the relaxation that self-laughter will bring you. Remember that often our foolish acts endear us most to others.

Ida Lupino told us the following story to demonstrate how a ludicrous accident can work to your benefit. Ida and twenty-eight other girls were all auditioning for George Bernard Shaw for a part in his play **Heartbreak House.** It was in the heat of summer and Ida, a frightened young teenager at the time, was the last to be called. She had plenty to opportunity to fret and she kept combing nervously at her blond hair.

Finally she found herself standing before Mr. Shaw. He gave her a long, surprised stare and then said tersely, "Go ahead, read."

Ida got through the part somehow. She knew she wasn't doing well. The other girls were all more professional than she. So she was astonished when, at the end of her reading, Mr. Shaw said, " Any girl who will go to such extremes to get a job deserves it. You have the role."

Ida didn't know what he was talking about. So she thanked him timidly and left.

On the way out she happened to pass a mirror and glanced at her reflection. She couldn't believe her eyes. The heat of the day had melted the lipstick in the bottom of her purse and her comb had become smeared with it. Her blond hair was streaked with bright red.

George Bernard shaw, thinking she had purposely chosen this eccentric approach to land a job, had rewarded her for her "imagination."

Ida sat down and laughed at herself until she cried. Now, whenever she finds herself faced with a difficult situation, she reminds herself of that first audition with Shaw.

Look back at your own life. Haven't there been times when a little unexpected humor, even at your own expense, would have helped you through a difficult situation? Haven't there been times when a little humor on your part might have eased the atmosphere and enabled you to play your role with more self-confidence?

Make a practice of allowing this saving grace of humor to demonstrate itself in all your future relationships. It will not only enable you to display your self more effectively but will also relax tensions among your fellow actors in the play of life.

eleven

Conflict

CONFLICT IN THE BUSINESS WORLD

IF We regard our jobs only as the necessary means of earning a living, we have not discovered the true satisfaction which comes from playing our roles to the fullest.

"Life really can be as sporting as any game we watch so breathlessly from the grandstands," says Charles Leonard, Michael Chekhov's editor and a playwright himself. "But one thing is important. You mustn't go tense into this conflict. You have to have a certain confidence, a sense of ease."

To help you discover this sense of ease, here are pointers from the professional acting world. Select those applicable to your problems.

HUNTING FOR A JOB?

A professional actor carefully reads the scripts offered him before deciding on a new role. You should be equally careful in choosing your future part in your play of life. A job is a necessary complement in helping you expand your role. Don't settle on one merely because it's easy or promises high monetary awards. Choose your life's work with this one important thought in mind: Is the work something I really want to do for its own sake?

SETTLE FOR LESS IN THE BEGINNING

Once you've decided on your goal don't be afraid to start at the bottom of the ladder. As long as your foot is firmly planted on the first rung you can make it to the top, and the knowledge you gain on the way will help to keep you up there once you've reached the peak.

Jack Lemmon points out that there are many personalities who, because of photogenic quality alone, rise quickly to the top in the film industry. But they never remain secure unless they acquire solid acting techniques. The same-the need for learning and experience--will hold true for you in the theatre of the world.

STUDY THE ROLE OF YOUR PROSPECTIVE EMPLOYER

Once you've decided on the kind of work you want to apply for, if possible, find out as much as you can about the man who will interview you. Draw up a little biography about him and review all the details until they become second nature to you.

This knowledge, which you will have made almost instinctive, will guide you in communicating with your prospective employer. It will also make him seem more familiar to you and therefore intimidating.

SOME PSYCHODRAMA

If you have a friend or a member of your family you can call upon to play the role of your prospective interviewer, you can apply the psychodrama as described in Chapter 9. Dr. Haas often uses this kind of psychodrama in his adult classes to help discouraged job seekers get an insight into the reasons for rejections.

Have your friend bounce your interview back to you several times. Listen to him with the ears of an employer and make the changes in your application that you feel should impress that employer.

If a partner for your psychodrama is unavailable, use a tape recorder, Record your application for a job and then after a day play it back. Listen attentively not just to what you said but how you said it. Are you apologetic, belligerent, tense or uncertain? Keep practicing until you are satisfied with the results.

HOW TO GROOM YOURSELF FOR THE INTERVIEW

Take a cue from the actor. He goes through the makeup and costume departments to prepare himself for his role. We urge to make the same careful preparations for your coming interview drama.

A man's costumes is relatively simple. He needs only to be neatly groomed.

Feminine costume's is somewhat more specific, since there are symbolic dresses for different professions. A woman applying for a job should first study, by observation, what the smart women of this profession are wearing. When a woman doesn't look the part, a prospective employer often will unconsciously reject her without even having considered her basic abilities.

This almost happened to Elke Sommer when she applied for a role in her first German picture.

Elke hadn't seen the script and she was young enough to imagine that a girl could get anywhere on sex appeal alone. She sailed into the audition room dressed like a siren.

The part, however, called for an innocent sixteen-year-old girl. The producers conducting the interview were ready to turn her down. Fortunately for Elke, the director present saw beneath her lurid makeup and she got the part.

"I also learned a good lesson," she told us, " Study the situation before you come to it, because most people aren't like that director. They judge only by what they see."

THE DAY OF THE INTERVIEW

Begin the important day of the interview by radiating self-confidence. See scintillating lights of various lively colors flashing through your body and circling you with their aura. Tell yourself that these sparkling lights issuing from you are the expression of your true worth. If a doubt does present itself send out your self-confident light to combat and destroy it. Make a game of this procedure.

WAITING FOR THE INTERVIEW

Often the prologue to an interview involves a long wait in an outer office. During this time your self-confidence, despite all your efforts, has tendency to evaporate.

To keep tension from mounting, Estelle Harman suggests the following exercise, which she gives to her young actors and actresses for use when they go for auditions.

Choose some activity in your life that is truly relaxing. It can be anything from listening to your favorite strains of music to looking at your favorite painting. Let us say it's strolling in a park.

Concentrate on the park until it actually comes alive. Then put yourself into it. Walk down your favorite path. Absorb yourself in this game so completely that your mind cannot flutter around anxiously.

You may not be able to maintain this concentration for longer than a moment. But in that moment you will have broken the chain of tension and restored your feeling of confidence.

NOW THE INTERVIEW

Your time has come. You walk into the office of your prospective employer. Faced with this situation, many people rush in like gangbusters, trying to exude dynamic drive and self-confidence. Unless you are a forceful individual you will give yourself completely away.

Here's a tip on how to approach the man you want to impress. It comes from Solly Baiano, head talent scout at Warner Brothers, who has a record of having picked a long list of eventual stars from among unknowns.

" An employer can spot a phony approach immediately and he resents it," Baiano, explained. "Each person should study himself and then present himself to show off his best qualities."

You can't do this, of course, if you're terrified of the man behind the desk, just as actors can't perform properly if they're intimidated by their audience.

AN ACTOR'S TRICK

Actors often play a game to bridge the initial tension when confronted by strangers. Montgomery Clift passed it on in a telegram to Karl Malden, who was terrified before opening in **All My Sons** in New York.

"Play the part as though everyone in the audience is naked," the telegram read.

It meant, Reduce everybody to the lowest common denominator -- his humanity -- and you'll see he's not so different form you, after all."

Once the man who is interviewing you is reduced to human proportions you will grow in your own self-confidence.

ANOTHER TRICK

This one was described for us by Mitzi Gaynor, who used it to overcome her panic while auditioning for the late Oscar Hammerstein II for the lead in **South Pacific.** She had never met Mr. Hammerstein and was in complete awe of him. She worke up that morning with a hacking cough. She had to clear her throat constantly.

In this paralyzing condition she found herself on the platform. She was convinced she couldn't possibly sing a note.

About to give up, she called on the self she had been developing through years of theatrical training. She sent that self out of her shoes where it stood dispassionately facing her.

"I want this part, I can do this part," Mitzi imagined that self telling her. "You don't really have a hoarse throat. It's all an excuse. But whatever you think about it, **this** me wants to perform."

"Then you perform," Mitzi replied to her self. And she imagined that confident self stepping back into her shoes and taking over.

Immediately her hacking cough disappeared. The energy she had wasted to create it flowed instead into her performance. She went through her numbers with such elan that Mr. Hammerstein signed her.

If your fear rises to panic proportions, take time out to turn the problem over to your self as Mitzi did. Relinquish all responsibility to it. You will discover that this act relaxes you immediately.

THE INTERVIEW

As the interview begins, don't rush through a set speech. Remember this is a drama, not an elocution class. The man who is interviewing you is your fellow player. Study him with quiet alertness.

If you have discovered anything of his background, see how it fits in with the image of the man behind the desk. Then try the " use of specifics" exercise which we have given you in Chapter 9 to establish rapport with him.

In the interview proper, follow the important rule Jeff Corey teaches his students: Don't ask yourself, How am I doing? Ask instead, What am I doing? This will center your mind on your goal instead of on yourself.

SO YOU DIDN'T GET THE JOB

If you don't get the job, don't tell yourself in despair that you lack what it takes. A rejection means little unless you accept it personally as a critical comment on you.

Solly Baiano remembers the day he took Burt Lancaster to Warner Brothers and introduced him to the head of his department. It was obvious the head wan't even mildly interested. As Solly and Burt were leaving, the man called Solly back.

"Why do you bring me these guys?" he complained. "This isn't an actor. He's an acrobat."

Burt went on to movie frame, and eventually won an Oscar, by refusing to don the limiting mask this appraisal had handed him.

You can do the same.

Check your interview to eliminate any flaws you may find, and try again elsewhere. Keep trying with self-confidence and eventually you'll find the employer and the right job meant for you.

NOW YOU HAVE IT

Once the job is yours, don't stop playing your role imaginatively. Don't allow yourself to forget your ultimate goal in the welter of everyday chores. Otherwise you will slip into a rut.

ARE YOU ALREADY IN THAT RUT?

To find out whether you're in that rut, look back to the day when you first applied for this job. After years of work do you still find yourself performing in a limited position? What has happened to all your youthful dreams? Have you fulfilled them?

If not, determine to fulfill them now. It's never too late. Change doesn't come from outer circumstances but from the heart.

"Anything you want to be you have to pretend to be at first," we were told by Cary Grant, who has proved the infallibility of this law. "Then you will become it. But you will become it more truly and quickly in direct ratio to the amount of life and feeling you put into your pretense."

Here is how A.C. Lyles, using Cary Grant's method, rose from a messenger boy in the Paramount mail department, to become a successful producer.

Lyles did his work in the department efficiently but not as a mere messenger boy. In his imagination he was already a producer, a man more interested in the welfare of the studio which would eventually market his products than in the money and power such a rule might bring him.

In those days a steady stream of visitors poured over the movie lot. The mailroom boys were given the chore of showing them around. It was a thankless job because few of the visitors tipped. The boys were glad to relinquish this onerous duty on Lyles.

Lyles took a different approach, the approach a producer might take toward showing off the studio in which he had a deep interest. He gave every visitor a deluze tour, carefully explaining all the details of movie-making familiar to him.

The visitors were delighted. They tried to press tips on him. But as an important "producer" Lyles wasn't interested. He asked them instead to drop a note to Y. Frank Freeman, then head of Paramount, voicing their appreciation. They complied.

Y. Frank Freeman became curious about this outstanding messenger boy who was mentioned in so many notes. He began calling on Lyles whenever he wanted special jobs done.

Presently Lyles graduated from the mailroom to the publicity department. Here again he did his work efficiently, always as the "producer" he longed to become. Meanwhile because of his attitude he made many friends among actors and actress.

When he eventually reached his goal and became a producer, these players were delighted to appear in his pictures.

Practice the magic "as if" in your work, too. It will waken the deep self within you to the realization that things are being done to allow for a fuller expression of life. And it will cooperate by opening channels through which ideas for improving your work will easily flow to you.

IS FEAR KEEPING YOU TENSE?

Sometimes fear of the unknown restrains us from playing a more expansive role in life. Such fear affects many professional performers, too. The successful ones have learned that the best way to fight fear is to accept every challenge. This is why you see Jack Lemmon not only in comedy roles but in such serious parts as the alcoholic in **Days of Wine and Roses.**

"If I like a part but turn it down just because I'm worried I many bomb out in it, I know I won't be able to look at myself in the mirrcr next morning," he told us. "You have to learn to tackle the things that are crushing you, not run from them."

To discover whether fear is influencing your important decisions, ask yourself these questions: Do I turn down interesting assignments and responsibilities on a flimsy excuse? Do I refuse a new job with a wider outlook solely because I fear the risk of executing a new task? Do I purposely refrain from doing anything unique in my present work for fear of calling attention to myself?

If these questions are answered in the affirmative you're allowing fear of failure to relegate you to the background.

THE REMEDY

Often we need only a little jolt to shove us out of a habitual negative mood into a positive one. This simple suggestion should help you cultivate the feeling of success.

Upon waking in the morning, savor all the **positive** things you accomplished the previous day. Dismiss the bloopers and inadequate performances entirely from your mind.

By concentrating on you virtues instead of your faults, you will learn to meet the daily challenges more constructively. And with time you will chalk up more important accomplishments.

Finally, you will have acquired enough self-confidence to accept that new and more expansive job when it is offered to you.

The following advice which the vital young actor, James Coburn received from Stella Adler, his well-known drama teacher, might be helpful.

"Find your capacities and live up to them," Coburn told us. "Allow yourself to attempt something even if it means failure. Make big mistakes if necessary. Remember your capacity for making mistakes is also your capacity for gaining successes. And if you keep your sights high and refuse to let failure intimidate you, in the end you will succeed."

EMPLOYEE RELATIONSHIPS

Sometimes, no matter how congenial your work is, you may find yourself harassed by some of your fellow employees. Today, this is such a recognized hazard that some firms are beginning to hold classes in psychodrama to improve relations among their employees.

If these is no such arrangement in your office, try the methods described in Chapter 9, "The Art of Human Understanding," to help you establish harmony with an uncongenial fellow worker.

THE JUST PLAIN HOSTILE PERSON

If, despite your sincere efforts to make peace, your fellow worker remains hostile, you may be justified in assuming he enjoys carrying a chip on his shoulder.

The best way to deal with this kind of actor on the stage of life is not to respond in kind to his hostility. Instead, look at the situation dispassionately. Ask yourself why he needs to show hostility. By treating the situation as an academic problem instead of an emotional one you prevent sparks from flying. The most hostile person tends to grow more amenable under such conditions. He will often become cooperative.

WHAT ABOUT THE CARPERS?

Practice the same dispassionate aloofness towards unwarranted criticism. By perpetually defending and justifying yourself you are merely presenting the other fellow with the opportunity to make his bow on your stage and in your play. Learn to do what the good actor does-simply ignore the heckler in the balcony.

Ron Worely, former assistant to Premier Bennett of British Columbia and presently public relations man for the British Columbia Ferry Authority, follows this motto in dealing with an unfair critic. "There's only so much wind in every storm. So batten down the hatches and ride it out."

THERE ARE ALWAYS DAYS

No matter how constructively you approach your work there may be days when you are assailed by self-doubts, by feelings of inadequancy a anxiety, even by grief of a personal nature. These moods come to us all. The professional actor has his share of them, too. He has to cope with them, however, for early in his career he has learned that under no conditions should he disappoint an audience which has paid money to see his perform.

THE SHOW MUST GO ON

"The show must go on" -This is the simple creed the theatrical world has articulated for its professionals. Illness, depression or grief are not considered excuses for missing a performance.

Thelma Ritter recalls watching an acrobat sail through a flawless routine of intricate and arduous feats with an expression of great pleasure. Later, she saw him collapse in agony from rheumatism he had been suffering the whole time. He didn't think he was doing anything unusual in playing his part to perfection despite his pain.

Periods of depression aren't limited to those who are having a hard struggle. Self-doubts and gloom visit even the most successful among us.

Anne Bancroft, secure in her acting profession, winner of two Tonies and an Oscar, told us, "There are many days when I'm struck with absolute sterility. Nothing happens and I can't make it happen. I'm completely lost. Sometimes it lasts a whole week. Then it's very frightening. But I've learned to put the problem in its proper perspective. I tell myself it's nothing so shattering I can't see my way through with discipline."

YOU AND YOUR MOODS

When you are faced with such moods on the stage of life, how do you react to them? Do you feel responsibility to your public and your fellow players? Or do you just cave in and visit your mood of self-pity on those around you?

Ida Lupino told us of two stenographers who came to her home to take dictation when she had to get a screenplay written on deadline. The first stenographer, instead of attending to business, kept up a running commentary of petty excuse and complaint.

Ida picked up the girl's nervousness and had to stop work before the day was over. When she reviewed her written material she was so mortified at its poor quality that she could not return to it for several days.

The next stenographer she employed was a calm, self-confident young woman. In her presence ideas began to tumble out of Ida's mind. She worked zestfully until late evening and her output was excellent.

After the work was finished and the stenographer was relaxing over a cocktail, she told Ida she had received such terrible news the night before she hadn't been able to sleep. When

Ida asked her how, under the circumstances, she could have remained so calm all day the girl replied simply:

"This is my living. So I've learned to discipline myself. When I set off for work I close that little door and pull the curtain on it all."

Which stenographer do you resemble in the role you play daily? If you are upset by a bad mood or depressing news, have you learned to close the little door. When you go to work? If not, try it. You will find in yourself a new self-respect for not inflicting your unhappiness on your fellow workers.

You'll discover, too, that by concentrating on your work you will be helping to alleviate the painful situation.

DR. THEATER

Actors have experienced the phenomenon of relief when they force themselves onto the stage, whatever their personal feelings. This is why they've come to dub the theater "Dr. Theater." Rex Harrison explained it to us this way:

"No matter how difficult it is to do, Dr. Theater requires you to put on your makeup and get into your role and go out there and face the public. It's hard, but you learn presently from experience that it's the one sure cure for whatever is troubling you. This is because the energy you've been spending on destructive emotions is channeled into constructive acting. And even if you don't leave the stage completely revived, you at least have a warm sense of fulfillment at having done your role creditably."

CHARLES LAUGHTON

Here is how a true professional—the late Charles Laughton—took Dr. Theater's prescription for a cruel black mood, which struck him as he and Bob Gist were completing a play for tour. Laughton and Gist had just attended the first of six dress rehearsals. They left the theater together, both thoroughly exhausted.

Over his martinis that night Laughton, almost crying with shame, began to cast accusations at himself.

"I've staged it very badly, you can see that," he told Gist. "I've bungled everything and I'm on the verge of destroying the careers of three superb actors. Before it's too late we ought to junk the whole thing, pay everyone off and forget it."

Gist wondered if the actor really meant what he was saying. He never found out. The next day, without a mention of the previous night Laughton was back at the theater, finishing the job he'd set himself.

HOW ABOUT YOU?

Train yourself in discipline by making a point of meeting and handling small annoyances as they appear, instead of avoiding them. Each day try to choose one unpleasant but necessary chore to clear up. It's not the large duties that you know you must do, but the little nagging matters that are most effective as discipline builders.

Your acquired store of discipline will sustain you in times of crisis. It can change what at first looks like a hopeless situation into a promising challenge. And you will find yourself accepting that challenge enthusiastically instead of allowing yourself to be crushed by it.

twelve

Voice

VOICE: ONE OF YOUR MOST IMPORTANT ASSETS

DO YOU realize the part voice plays in conducting your role in life? Stop and listen to the voices around you. How does a whining or a nasal or a harsh delivery affect your ears? And how do you respond to the expressive well-modulated tones of a person who has learned to speak properly?

ACTORS AND VOICE

For an illustration of the important role voice plays in presenting an image to the outside world, let us go back to the days of transition from silent to talking films.. Many romantic stars of the silent film were suddenly swept into oblivion by the new medium.

Why? They were betrayed by shrill, ugly or high-pitched voices. Their places were taken by stage actors with trained voices. Today voice is considered so important to an actor's education that the major film studios all employ voice teachers for their young players.

OTHER PROFESSIONS AND VOICE

Voice cultivation is not limited to the professional actor. Even the most capable political has difficulty winning an election if his delivery is poor. Ministers, priests or rabbis with unpleasant or monotonous voices seldom get their messages across effectively to their congregations.

A doctor's bedside manner depends in good part on his ability to convey confidence by the sound as well as the meaning of his words.

The need of a trained voice in these professions has long been recognized. But today intelligent businessmen are beginning to realize the importance of voice in their work, too. Some of them take instruction to enable them to deliver important speeches dynamically, arouse enthusiasm in their salesmen, or convince reluctant board members to adopt new ideas.

YOU AND YOUR VOICE

Do you present a confident image to the world—until you open your mouth? Do you speak with a monotonous delivery when you most need a dynamic voice to present a fine idea? Do you confuse repellent tension in your voice with relaxed enthusiasm?

Are you carrying the dialect of the country in which you grew up, even though this dialect may be harsh and brittle to the ear? Are you faithfully mirroring the faulty diction you learned from parents and early teachers, who in turn learned it from their parents?

If so, change. Give your voice a chance to be its natural self and express you at your finest.

YOU WON'T LOOK PHONY

We often become so accustomed to our habitual voices that we feel self-conscious at the mere thought of changing. We fear it will make us sound artificial and "stuck up."

It may comfort you to know that professional actors sometimes suffer the same qualms at the beginning of their careers.

When Tony Curtis first entered pictures, proper speech sounded unnatural to him because all his life he had spoken "Brooklynese." He confided to Estelle Harman, his drama coach, that he felt changing his voice would be an act of betrayal to his own background and his own people.

Tony had to be convinced this was wrong thinking. Then he put his whole heart into voice cultivation. Today there isn't a trace of the "Brooklynese" of his childhood.

SOME POINTERS

Because of the important role voice plays in life, we asked Miss Gertrude Fogler to give us a few important pointers on its cultivation. Miss Fogler, a former actress and one of Hollywood's most famous voice instructors, has been employed for many years by Metro-Goldwyn-Mayer studios. She has trained most of the stars who have been under contract to the studio, ranging from Leslie Caron to Ava Gardner. Many of them, such as Sophia Loren, Cesare Danova, Elke Sommer and Ricardo Montalban, had serious accent as well as voice problems to overcome.

You will find Miss Fogler's suggestions valuable in gaining new insight into the mechanism of speech. Perhaps you will also be encouraged to start a more thorough development of this important asset, which is so valuable in performing your role in life with distinction.

CULTIVATED VOICE

A cultivated voice is one which flows easily and naturally without strain.

"The idea is to make music as much as possible out of speech," Miss Fogler told us. "And everyone who has hearing can do it, because we all possessed an instinctive knowledge of the art when we were babies."

Most of us have lost this talent in adulthood simply because we have acquired the erroneous idea that the entire speech mechanism depends on our conscious control, It doesn't.

"The human voice has no need of being manipulated to turn breath into tone," explains Miss Fogler. "It has an innate ability to perform this miracle of its own accord. The thought of tone alone is sufficient to produce tone."

TONE STARTS AT THE LARYNX

The production of tone starts at the larynx in our throats. It is here than breath is turned into the vibration that is tone. When we misuse our larynx to pronounce our vowels from our throats we interface with the natural production of tone. The result is forced, harsh, or nasal speech.

The remedy is simple. Just relax the throat and let the vibrations of air which form the tone progress unhampered to your mouth. Here your lips and tongue should take over the complete responsibility of forming the words.

Imagine a taut pipeline stretching from your diaphragm, which lies just under your rib cage, to your mouth This imaginary line must be pictured as taut because such a picture will help you to achieve the concentrated force which gives the voice power. As the air passes through this line, imagine that it is being charged with vibration (tonal) qualities at the larynx. Then see it releasing into your mouth in tiny bubbles. Be sure you see those bubbles passing under the bridge of your palate instead of over it through your nose.

LET YOUR TONGUE AND LIPS DO THE WORK

As each bubble comes to the tip of your tongue have your tongue and lips convert it into a word and then release it.

Don't force the words or thrash around to get them out. Treat the air bubbles delicately with your tongue and lips. Remind yourself that speaking is like working with cobwebs. You don't need heaviness of approach.

Learn to have faith in the efficiency of your tongue to take care of its chore. It was created for this purpose.

You may be self-conscious at first about putting the tongue in full charge of shaping your words, because you have grown accustomed to forcing speech from your throat. If so, try to imagine your tongue encased in a rubber glove such as electricians wear when handling electric wires. Tell your-self that the tongue in its glove is insulated against making mistake. You will be delighted at the increased sense of confidence this image will give you.

SAVOR YOUR WORDS

Take time when you speak. Don't rush your words. Enjoy them. While you are fashioning each bubble of air into a word savor it fully as if it were a delicious morsel. Give it love before you release it to the outside world. To be alive and vibrant, every word must be impregnated with the vitality of creation.

Here is another image that may help you. Picture your larynx as a lighthouse in which a gleaming lamp is hung. The radiance from this lamp pours into your mouth and there is translated by tongue and lips into rays of light to be cast outward over the ocean of life.

You would no dram of throwing the lighthouse lamp into the ocean to illuminate it. So you should not constantly be hurting the lamp in your throat outward alongwith the beams of tone it is emitting.

By studying any good book of diction you can find the correct placement of tongue and lips to pronounce each vowel and consonant. Make a game of this study and practice your placements faithfully, so that your tongue may get practice at its new chores. Always keep in mind these two rules:

1. Don't interfere with your throat muscles. Let your larynx take full charge of changing air into vibration (tone).

2. Transform tone into words with our mouth and lips alone. It is their chore.

FEELING

If you practice the preceding rules you should achieve an easy, unstrained method of speech. This, however, is not enough. We all know of stage actors whose excellent control of speech and diction fills us with intellectual admiration but leaves us emotionally cold. On the other hand, actors like the late Charles Laughton have the power to stir us profoundly. What ingredient have they added to their perfect speech? Feeling. Feeling gives the voice expression and meaning.

As children we knew instinctively how to register emotion with our voices. Then as we grew into adulthood and became more preoccupied with mental pursuits, we came to regard the voice as a vehicle to express ideas alone.

But the most uplifting idea in the world expressed in dry intellectual accents will not stir people or rally them to your cause. You **must** employ feeling to get across your meaning. It is feeling that puts nuances and inflections into our speech, lending it color and rhythm and subtle meanings.

Pronounce these simple sentences in a monotone. It's a very nice day. How do you do? I'm so glad you came." They convey nothing. Now repeat them with varying inflections. "It is a **very** nice day. I'm so glad you came." By changing your feeling about the day and your visitor you convey different meanings.

However, emotion, like tone, is something that we cannot consciously manufacture. We must learn to leave the channels open and let it express itself through tone.

FEELING AND TONE

Tone is not something you change to make room for emotion. Express yourself in terms of tone as a dancer expresses himself in terms of bodily movements. A dancer doesn't think of substituting feeling for the body through which he must express that feeling. He knows he cannot. What he does is to increase the artistic value of his body by graceful movement.

In the same way you must think in terms of increasing the value of tone, which is air vibration, by giving that tone substance, vitality and expression.

How do you go about it? A little physiological information may help you. The solar plexus is a bundle of nerves which lies just below the diaphragm. It is the focal point of your central nervous system.

If you want to convey feeling in your voice, you must experience that feeling first in your solar plexus. Once you have aroused feeling there, you need not worry about how it will express itself. Nature will take care of it for you.

Just fashion the emotion-charged bubbles of air that enter your mouth into the appropriate words with your tongue and lips.

If you cannot feel the emotion at once, follow the methods described in Chapter 6, "Emotion," to waken the required feeling in your solar plexus. Once you have roused it strongly there, you will have no trouble channeling it into your voice.

VOLUME

Have you ever suffered this disconcerting experience? When you are speaking with one or two persons and do not need to "raise" your voice, all goes well. But the minute it is necessary to speak more loudly the old strain returns.

You hear yourself shouting. Your voice gives the impression of aggressiveness or shrewishness. If you keep up the shouting for any length of time your throat becomes hoarse with the strain.

It is not necessary to yell to make yourself heard. Again, the fault lies in taking on an operation which should be turned over to nature. If you cooperate she will provide you with sufficient volume to throw your voice farther than by shouting, and without any strain.

How is this done? Once more we must turn to physiology. Our body is divided into an upstairs and downstairs by the diaphragmatic muscle. This important muscle, which we have mentioned before, forms a strong arched shelf just under our ribs and protects the lungs from the pressure of the abdominal muscles which might crush them without this safeguard.

All of our forceful movements originate below our diaphragm. Here, too, volume originates as a kind of stretch tension which we draw up through our feet. The secret, then, is to relax only above the diaphragm, so that the life force can enter from below.

INCREASING LIFE ENERGY FOR VOLUME

If you want to observe a practical example of how stretch tension is transformed into power, look at a baseball pitcher. He increases his life energy by planting his left foot firmly against the earth and then by drawing that energy up through his body to the palm that holds the ball.

Now imagine your diaphragm as a gigantic palm holding the ball of air which is to be converted into tone at your larynx and transformed into words by your tongue and lips. You will find that by tightening your muscles below the diaphragm, and especially by using pressure in your feet, you can increase your volume without tension.

Caruso, the great singer, knew well the secret of drawing in life energy and converting it into the magnificent volume of voice that made him famous.

"How do you support your tone?" he was asked.

'With my feet, of course," Caruso replied.

Try it. It may take practice, for most of us have allowed the diaphragmatic muscle to become flabby through disuse.

Plant your feet firmly and stretch, drawing the life energy from the center of the earth up through your feet to your diaphragm.

Then allow it to release naturally through the taut imaginary airline which leads from that muscle shelf to your mouth. You will be pleasantly surprised at the amount of volume at your disposal without the least strain to throat or vocal bands.

WHY NOT GO FARTHER?

We have given only a few rules here which, if carefully followed, will improve your voice. Miss Fogler has this additional suggestion for those with only a modest income but a strong desire to continue this fascinating and rewarding study.

Why not get together a group of your friends and engage a voice teacher? In this way the fees will be reduced and you will have the pleasure and the profit of working together. Certainly, the dividends will pay you many times over for your trouble. You will discover that a pleasing and vital voice increases your self-confidence a hundredfold and helps to give a more dynamic performance on the stage of life.

thirteen

Cliches

WHAT IS A CLICHE?

IN DICTIONARIES we learn that a cliche is a trite phrase that has lost precise meaning by iteration or a hackneyed or stereotyped expression.

Cliches on the stage are committed, as a rule, by lazy actors. By using gestures and facial expressions so stereotyped they have become symbolic of certain states of emotion or processes of thought, these actors are able to portary the feeling of their characters without any creative effort.

We, on the stage of life, are just as apt to rely on cliches to express ourselves, But cliches are of the past and represent the deadwood of thinking. The more you root them out of your life and play your role with imagination the more vital will be your performance. We therefore felt you would be interested in a chapter dealing exclusively with the most common cliches and giving suggestions on how they may be avoided.

EMOTION

When a stereotyped rendition of genuine emotion is portrayed, that is a cliche. There is no need to discuss it futher here, as emotion has been dealt with thoroughly in Chapter 6.

Cliches of speech in themselves are not necessarily harmful. "How are you," "Glad to see you," and so forth serve as symbols of expression to make life move along more easily. In this respect such cliches are actually helpful.

But when we make an inordinate use of such shopworn expressions as "That's the way the cooky crumbles," "I have news for you," "That I'll buy," "It's yea big," et cetera, we hamper the very ideas we wish to express. Through long usage most of these phrases have little meaning at all.

Sometimes a perfectly good idea is rejected because we have used an especially irritating cliche to project it.

To discover if you are guilty of relying on cliches try out this exhilarating and profitable experiment. Play watchdog over yourself for an hour or two. When you find yourself about to utter a cliche, refrain. Instead, substitute an original phrase or sentence in its place.

If you are an habitual cliche-user you may find this exercise difficult at first. But practice it faithfully and you will presently discover that your thinking has grown sharper and clearer. Your honesty of approach will attract more attention to you.

You will also make, another pleasant discovery. Once your unconscious realizes that you are genuinely interested in expressing yourself imaginatively, it will begin to provide you with phrases which are refreshingly original. Be careful when these phrases do come to you, not to use them more than twice in a single conversation, even though they elicit approval form your audience.

Each time you repeat an original phrase it becomes less original until finally it can degenerate into a cliche, too. Trust to your unconscious to provide you with fresh phrases when the need arises. Your unconscious can be depended on if you keep the channels clear.

GESTURE

Closely related to speech cliches are gesture cliches. On stage they are referred to as "indicating" acting. According to Mark Robson, well-known film director and archfoe of all cliches, this is the worst kind of acting and should be avoided.

At the beginning of his career Napoleon Bonaparte was guilty of this kind of "indicating" acting, which made him look much like a comic opera figure. Writer Walter Reisch tells the whimsical story of how Bonaparte transformed this inept image of himself into that of powerful emperor.

It seems that when Napoleon began cutting his conqueror's swath across Europe he became very self-conscious of the figure he projected. He was short, potbellied, with small eyes, long ears, an awkward walk, and the ebullient gesticulations of an Italian.

Napoleon went to the famous French actor Francois Joseph Talma, who was his close friend, and asked how he could create a better image of himself. Together they worked on the problem. Talma realized that Napoleon's nervous gestures were emphasizing all his negative qualities. He suggested that the Little Corporal keep his right hand in his coat whenever he was in public. This would serve two purposes. It would anchor Napoleon's right, most expressive hand. It would act as a constant reminder to keep the left hand motionless.

So successful was the stance in creating a distinctive image for Napoleon that today it is regarded as the hallmark of a cold' autocratic emperor.

You do not need to anchor your hand in your coat or otherwise eliminate gestures. They are valuable when used to emphasize a point or to indicate receptivity of another's viewpoint' since they send out a charge like a current of electricity that flows from you to the man whom you wish to impress and then back again, thus establishing rapport between you. But when you overload your conversation with gestures or use a cliche gesture, the current is weakened by familiarity.

Be on guard against cliche gestures. Weed them out, and as you did with phrases, let your unconscious mind originate fresh ones.

You will find yourself making a far more forceful impression on others. But as in the case of verbal cliches, remember that any original gesture, if overused, tends to become a cliche of your own.

WARDROBE

Sometimes a startling innovation of dress or makeup in films will spill over into real life and develop into a cliché. During the Egyptian era young girls painted their eyebrows to their hairline a la Elizabeth Taylor as Cleopatra. For a while actors in Italian films wore dark glasses even at night. Dark glasses suddenly became the fashion among moviegoers.

"Audrey Hepburn wears Capri pants for a role in a movie and any number of women take up the style, even though it may be unbecoming to them," Mark Robson told us. "There's nothing that makes a person look more like a sheep than to adopt slavishly a wardrobe cliche."

The clothes you see on the screen were designed to accent the personality of a particular woman in a particular movie. Instead of mimicking those clothes, do for yourself that the studio costume designers did for the star. Experiment until you find the style that will enhance your own individuality.

SITUATION

Situation cliches in films are used for a variety of purposes. Sometimes they are necessary to illustrate part of the plot, to bridge over gaps created by censorship problems, or simply to titillate the audience. But when they are carried over into real life by moviegoers they become deadly situation Sliches in our daily living.

"Much of the blame for so many disvorces among young people is due to the screen, I'm convinced," writer Stanley Shaporo said. " Many couples expect life to be the way it is in movies. And when they don't find it so they feel jilted and break up. They don't realize that the whole setup is phony—just a pleasant cliche."

Even when we don't go so far as to get a divorce because the script of our life isn't following our favorite scenario, we can nevertheless be guilty of situation cliches. To find out whether you are reacting to situations organically or with cliches ask yourself these questions.

Am I concerned chiefly about whether I have acceptable emotions, whether I am putting on the right face for others, or am I turning all my attention on the situation itself?

Much of the energy and originality which we could bring to our problems is blocked by our habitual use of cliche responses, because we believe they are "acceptable."

If this is happening to you, try to take your mind off yourself and your reactions and concentrate completely on the situation and the means of solving it. Such action tends to eliminate tensions and disorganized emotions. If these two symptoms reappear it means you have fallen back into the old cliche reactions.

Check yourself and get back to your problem again By making a practice of this exercise you will become more and more proficient at handling situations. Best of all, you will begin to accept tham as exciting challenges instead of menacing dangers.

You will discover, too, that your unconscious can be trusted to help you whenever you tackle a problem imaginatively and constructively.

PERSONALITY

Perhaps America's greatest personality cliche is epitomized in the hero of Western movies. While the chief villain in these pictures is always erudite, Mark Robson pointed out to us, the hero is seldom well-educated. he isn't quick with his tongue and does a lot of bashful dirt-kicking as he searches for the words to kame himself understood. But he has deep, true feelings, and when pushed hard enough, finally moves into action and defeats the villian.

The cliche of the homespun illiterate, rich in heart and feeling, springs from the history of early America when there was a scarcity of educated men in this country. The average person was a farm boy who looked at education with a mixture of envy and suspicion.

However, the fact that Europe has taken the Western to her heart proves that there is much to be said for the honest, relaxed, homespun approach.

It is possible to get across the idea of solid common sense and homespun loyalty without falling into the cliches of Western hero casting. It isn't necessary to drawl, or act bashful in the presence of superior learning while simultaneously conveying your distrust of the learned person.

When you view painting, for instance, you don't need to comment, " Well, I'm no expert in art but I like this." Simply state what you like about it. Your opinion is as good as the next fellow's. Then listen attentively while he explains his feelings. It may be that he **is** an expert in the field, in which case you needn't feel ashamed or defensive about your lack of knowledge. Just play the scene in a relaxed way, focusing your attention on what he is saying. Thus you will be educating yourself the easyway and flattering him as well.

On the other hand, you may have a fine education and a quick mind that knows the answers even before the questions are asked. If this is the case, you might want to tone down your smartness and inject a pleasant homespun solidity into your personality. It makes for better relationship with others.

Learn to take time before you reply to any question even though you may know the answer immediately.

George Stevens, director of such movies as **Giant** and **Shane** has earned the reputation on being a fascinating man because he has learned the art of thoughtful receptivity. Mr. Stevens simply allows a lot of conversation to flow around him before he opens his mouth on any subject, though he may have his reply ready almost from the beginning. But his measured and careful responses convince others that he is a man who thinks things through rather than sounding off glibly from the top of his head.

IDEAS

Idea cliches are the most harmful of all because they have the power to warp and cramp our individuality. Such ideas are the traditional "truths" whose only claim to legitimacy is that they have always been with us.

If you suspect you are prone to cliche thinking, check yourself the next time you are in a gathering. Do you tend to go along with the general trend of thinking expressed in the conversation? Do you even search for additional material to add to what is being said, though privately you do not agree with that opinion?

Do you stop and weigh the conversation, decide what you agree with and what you disagree with, and then voice your opinion regardless of what the majority opinion is?

If you have never indulged in this fascinating kind of acting, why not try it? Don't raise your points belligerently or arbitrarily. Put to use the play-acting techniques that you have learned in this book and express what you really think.

You will find it exhilarating to go against the general current. Moreover, if you state your beliefs in a reasonable manner, you will find people beginning to look up to you as a person of integrity. Best of all, you will discover this weighing of your own beliefs tends to clarify all your thinking and widen your horizons.

CRUELTY IS A CLICHE

On the other hand, do not confuse expressing your opinions reasonably with the cliche of "frankness." and express it by being brutally cruel.

Brutality and anger are the oldest of our cliches, for they spring from, our caveman days and bear the stamp of over century-old repetition. It is easy to react in cruel and domineering ways to the challenges that life presents us.

But how much better if we deliberately choose a constructive and imaginative approach to meet these challenges. Robson calls it "playing **with** the scene" as distinguished from just "playing the scene." And he gives this arresting example to illustrate his point.

After a harrowing near miss, a young husband asks his wife to keep their small son out of the driveway of their home at the hour of his return from work so that the child's life will not be in jeopardy. The wife promises, but one day forgets. The husband turns his car into the driveway, runs over and kills his child.

There are, as Robson points out, two ways for the husband to play the ensuing scene. The easiest is the cliche. He berates his wife, accusing her of murdering their child and tears her to shreds to assuage the pentup fury and grief within himself. This is what he calls "playing the scene," that is, allowing the scene to take its natural course, carrying you along with it.

The second method is much harder to execute, for it consists of handling the scene rather than allowing oneself to be handled by it. In this version the man stifles his own grief and his brutal urge for vengeance—the cliche reaction to such a catastrophe—to put on a far nobler act. Realizing his wife's suffering, he makes every effort to comfort her. The man who plays **with** the scene in this way gains a moral victory over himself and eliminates the possibility of future remorse and self-incrimination after his urge to destroy has spent itself.

Fortunately, most of us are not faced with such a brutal situation in our daily living. But how often in lesser ways have we indulged in cruel "frankness" at the expense of others? Next time play the scene constructively. Put yourself in the other person's shoes and look at life from his viewpoint. Then play **with** the scene. It takes consummate skill, out it's worth the challenge, for it brings healing rather than hurt to those with whom we are in contact.

WAR: THE ULTIMATE CLICHE

If brutality in any form is a cliche, then, as Robson pointed out to us, the most deadly cliche of our civilization is war. War was man's way of handling problems in the days when he had little or no intelligence and could not possibly have gained advantage by sitting around a conference table and trying to solve his problems rationally.

Today we can discuss our differences instead of fighting over them. But we still react with resigned cliche statements like, "It's no use. War will always be with us."

Why not, instead of thinking so fatalistically, put your self among the non-cliche people who are wholeheartedly endorsing the idea of peace as a workable phenomenon in our affairs?

Don't pay the idea of peace lip service only. Live it in your daily life. Using the techniques you find in this book, deliberately try to circumvent animosity and discord in your relations with your employer, your fellow workers, your family, friends and acquaintances.

Practice acting out of love and compassion. These are fresh ideas and they are vibrant with energy. They have the power hymblest of your chores into an exciting challenge. And they will help you play out your role in life imaginatively and successfully.

Why not at least try it, and see what happens in you?

MANNERISMS

We all tend to accumulate mannerisms. So clearly are we marked by them that the FBI can often nab a criminal through the knowledge of some petty mannerism when a photograph or a detailed description of his appearance is not available.

Mannerism usually spring from nervousness. And because they betray a sense of self-consciousness and tension they make an unpleasant impression.

Self-conscious mannerisms often accompany 1he telling of a joke. These spring from our uncertainty about whether it will be enthusiastically accepted or not. So it is will to remember that a joke comes over far better when it isn't "furred" by a mannerism.

Some common mannerisms are the constant set smile, even in the face of catastrophe, the slumped self-conscious posture and the continual crossing and uncrossing of arms and legs. the toying with rings or a pipe, even the gait. Be on guard for them.

THE FURNITURE ACTOR

One of the most prevalent of mannerisms is so familiar to the professional world that the guilty person is dubbed a "furniture actor." He's the actor who always leans against something or at least touches it. Without a prop to cling to he's like a turtle without its shell.

Practice the following method for contract acting on one person or another whenever you are in a gathering. It can be fun and it will bring results.

First look at the person with whom you wish to establish contact. Don't stare, just imagine your gaze is a fine but strong invisible wire which stretches from you to him. Imagine a current coursing along this wire toward him.

Now by concentration maintain this wire between you and him even though you may turn your back on him. Just change the focal point of the wire to suit your position. Let it, for instance, come out of the back of the head, or the left or right ear. Though you may no longer be looking at him, and to all appearances have put him out of mind, you will still be holding his attention.

As long as you keep that wire intact and the current flowing strongly through it, he will feel drawn to you even though he may believe you have forgotten him.

Once you have developed contact acting to a fine art you will find it makes a far deeper impression than any of the more obvious bids for attention.

EXERCISE 1 **This exercise comes from the well-known drama coach Kurt Conway, who has been teaching for**

fifteen years and whose pupils have included such popular performers as Tony Bill, Polly Bergen and Joanne Woodward.

Each day take an inventory of yourself. Don't make this a long introspection, for that tends to turn your thoughts too much inward. Spend just enough time-say, while you are walking or shopping or lunching—to examine your behavior objectively. Check yourself for mannerisms. Listen to your speech. When you find something you don't like, make a game out of concentrating on its elimination.

This sort of "personality checkup" can be made easier if you have the help of a friend, or better still a group of friends who can be trusted to be objective but not cruel in their criticisms.

Conduct a little fun session, as Kurt Conway sometimes does in his classes. Let each person do an imitation of another in the group. Physical and vocal mannerisms register quickly on others and the most outstanding of these mannerisms are utilized for the impersonations. Confronted with an impersonation of yourself, you will become graphically aware of your most obvious mannerisms. This is the first step to ridding yourself of them.

EXERCISE 2 **An exercise to train yourself in contact acting given by Mark Robson, who points out that it is the opposite of cliché acting. Those actors who know how to utilize contact acting can even draw attention to themselves when their backs are turned to their audience. Some past masters at contact acting are Cary Grant, Bing Crosby and Bob Mitchum.**

If you're a furniture actor, it means you lack the confidence to stand alone. The person with his mannerism can never create a dynamic impression. Here's an imaginative trick to help you conquer the habit. It comes from the Method School of acting, and if you've been studying Chapter 7, you will have sharpened your imaginative powers to the point where you can now put them to practical use.

Imagine yourself as a tall, majestic tree. Your feet are the roots, firmly planted in the soil. Your legs are sturdy twin trunks. They are strong enough to hold you up. You have no need to lean on anything.

You are the tallest, most secure being in the room, but since you are no longer human you have no need to compare yourself favorably or otherwise with those around you. As a tree you can look down benignly out of your highest branches at the phenomena of human life below you.

What is said or done down there cannot possibly hurt you, even if an unkind barb is thrown your way. You are a tree, and a tree cannot be injured by the sarcasms or criticisms of human beings. You are outside their sphere of action.

Make a game of putting yourself in the strong, yet benign image of this tree every time you want ot lean against something or feel for support. Presently you will find yourself cured of being a furniture actor.

TWO EXERCISES

Two exercises follow. The first is designed to help you root out mannerisms and cliches. The second gives you a form of magnetic uncliche acting which is practiced by many stars of stage and screen.

fourteen

Those Blemishes

HAVE YOU CONSIDERED PLASTIC SURGERY?

DO YOU dread facing the world because of some physical defect? When you are among people is your attention constantly drawn to that defect? Do you imagine that every eye is critically focused on it? Is it so disconcerting that you are unable to play your role on the stage of life with the necessary enthusiasm?

If you suffer from this kind of problem this is your special chapter.

First, look at yourself objectively. Is your defect a serious error of nature or the mutilating result of illness or accident? Whatever the case, there's hope for it.

In recent years plastic surgery has been used as a corrective for such gross defects. The sense of freedom from humiliation which surgery brings to the victims of disfigurements often makes the difference between a serious neurosis and buoyant mental health.

So if you have a disturbing facial disfigurement don't hesitate to take remedial measures. Consult your local hospital as to whether there are plastic surgeons on its staff, or ask your general physician to refer you to an expert in this field.

DEFECTS PLASTIC SURGERY CAN'T CURE

Sometimes plastic surgery cannot correct deep skin blemishes, such as massive birthmarks or ugly red scars from accidents. Yet today there is hope for people suffering from such disfigurements, too.

Gordon Bau, head of makeup at Warner Brothers Studios and president of the Society of Makeup Artists of Hollywood, told us that he receives many letters from people who had picked up his name from screen credits. They ask for help in curing their blemishes. Some even come to Hollywood to consult with him.

"I never turn down a request for help, because I know what a terrible burden disagreement can be," Bau told us. "And with today's improved makeup bases, I've never come across any case so desperate that it can't be helped."

One client of his was a fifteen-year-old girl from Northern California who had fallen into a threshing machine. Plastic surgery had remedied much of the damage, but it could not do away with the angry red scars that disfigured her face.

Bau prepared a makeup base which would successfully conceal those scars, and has been providing her with this base for a number of years. Thanks to his concern, the girl is today happily married and teaching, instead of living the withdrawn hermit's life her disfigurements could·otherwise have imposed on her.

Another otherwise beautiful sixteen-year-old girl was brought by her father from Australia to ask Bau if anything could be done to conceal an ugly birthmark covering half her face. It was so destructive to her emotionally, he explained, that she had even tried to commit suicide.

A makeup base that successfully covers the birthmark has freed the child of her terrible anguish. Today she is as normal as any teenager.

If an unsightly blemish is making your life miserable, consult an expert in the field of cosmetics. Camouflage makeup may be the answer to your need.

IRREGULARITIES OR FEATURE DEFECTS

Sometimes one faulty feature, especially in a woman, can mar an otherwise lovely face. Often the features may be regular but should be highlighted for emphasis. It may console you to know, if you are such a woman that even the glamor girls of screen and television need makeup to bring out their beauty.

Connie Stevens and Debbie Reynolds both require corrective makeup to give their eyes size and luminosity. Audrey Hepburn has beautiful doe eyes and an entrancing smile, but it takes makeup to bring out these qualities.

On the other hand, though Diane McBain has a beautiful face, it is too mute without specific makeup to high light its effectiveness.

So if you have irregular features, don't despair. The stars themselves aren't born perfect, but through the genius of the studio makeup departments they can be made to appear perfect even on wide screen, where in closeups a single eye can be. five feet high.

Books, magazines, and private consultants will give you practical advice on makeup. And when you find advice to change your appearance for the better, don't be too lazy to follow it. You will be surprised at how little effort it requires to transform yourself from a drab, uninteresting nonentity into an attractive person. And with the increased self-confidence that comes from knowing you are making a favourable impression on others, you will find yourself playing your role in life more effectively.

HOW ABOUT MEN'S HAIR STYLES?

Hair styles also are an important factor in making us look attractive. Women have beauty salons to rely on for hair style advice. Less attention is paid to the important role that the cut of the hair plays in bringing put the masculine personality.

Therefore we consulted Jay Sebring, one of Hollywood's most imaginative hair stylists. Sebring trims the hair of such stars as Henry Fonda, Frank Sinatra, Marlon Brando, Richard Burton, Gardner McKay and Bobby Darin.

Sebring doesn't limit himself to members of the film colony. Other professional and businessmen come to him, too. Clerks, filling station operators. and parking lot attendants are among his clients. Oil moguls from Texas pay him 500 dollars to fly to their homes to trim their hair. There has been so much demand for his imaginative haircuts that Sebring has now started a school for barbers.

When a man goes for hair styling, Sebring takes many things into account before designing a personalized haircut for him. He studies the structure of his client's face so that the haircut will properly balance his features. Sebring maintains that even the hair of one becoming bald can be cut in a way to camouflage its thinness. He also takes into account his client's profession as well as the image the man wants to project to the world.

Many of Sebring's customers tell him their whole outlook of life has been improved by these individualized haircuts. One of his most enthusiastic clients, actor Harry Guradino, put it this way: "It's two years of analysis in forty-five minutes."

Since barbers specializing in personalized haircuts for men are becoming more and more numerous, there may be one in your locality. If not, we suggest you consult with your own barber on your next visit, instead of letting him cut your hair in the same old way.

You may be surprised at his constructive suggestions. Don't be afraid to take them. Trying a change, even when it relates only to the cut of your hair, is good for the personality.

WOMEN, THIS IS FOR YOU

Most people have defects of figure as well as face. A little devotion to the subject of dress can bring great rewards in helping a woman conceal her faults and display her best image to the world. So we consulted Edith Head, chief designer for Paramount and winner of seven Academy Awards for her screen fashions, for some constructive hints.

"Fashion is now a science," Miss Head told us. "And with all the magazine, newspaper, radio and TV space devoted to the subject there's no excuse nowadays for an unattractive appearance."

This is Miss Head's do-it-yourself method of locating and correcting body faults:

Stand before a full-length mirror with a tape measure. Follow these two simple rules.

1. Analyze yourself with ruthless honesty, using your tape measure as guide.

2. Then take a page from Army practice and camouflage the faults. Here are a few camouflage pointers:

Big in hips and waist" Wear loose skirts and darker colors. Avoid patterns or shiny-surfaced fabrics.

Thick-waisted, or high -or low-waisted" Wear the loose two-piece garment that hides the waist effectsively.

Too fat or too thin? Wear loose-fitting clothes. Tight-fitting clothes show up either defect.

Stubby legs? Wear plain shoes and longer skirts regardless of "fashion length." Wear dull stockings one shade darker than your skin.

Bow legs? Follow the above rules for stubby legs plus seamless stockings and loose skirts so the hemline won't emphasize the bowed legs.

Ugly arms? If your upper arm is skinny or flabby, or if your elbows are bony, cover them.

"Make fashion secondary. Your first question should always be, 'Is it becoming to me?"

Try this method of shopping for clothes. Take along your second self as a companion. When your try on a dress, get out of yourself through the use of your imagination and into the shoes of that second self. Now examine your reflection in the mirror as if it were that of a stranger you're seeing for the first time.

Ask yourself: "Even if that dress is in the height of fashion, does it look right on the stranger in the mirror?" If not, refuse to buy it no matter what the saleslady says. There's nothing in the world so treacherous or self-defeating as feeling that your clothes don't fit properly or are inappropriate.

If you wish to study the subject of dress further you will find many good books, as well as current magazines, which deal with the subject.

ATTENTION, MEN!

Now we come to the question of how men should dress. Modern men are becoming more aware of fashion. Men, too, want garments that will hide figure faults and give them a sense of security in their relations with the world.

So we approached Sy Devore, Hollywood clothier, who acts as fashion consultant to many stars. He designs much of the masculine attire you see on the screen. The following are some of Devore's camouflage rules for a trimmer, more masculine appearance:

In choosing a suit, Devore suggests you select a style in which you feel the most comfortable unless it is entirely uncomplimentary to you. Whatever style you choose, it is possible to have the suit altered to take care of defects in your figure.

One shoulder higher than the other? This is a common fault. The tailor will use a little padding on the tip of the lower shoulder to build it up, but in a concave natural effect.

Hips thick, check thin? Your tailor can pad out the front of the coat with a haircloth lining to give the chest contour.

Thick waistline? Elvis Presley and John Waync have this problem, since both are heavy-set fellows. Devore suggests you wear the trousers low and snug about the waist. This holds in the stomach, whereas a high waist-line causes it to protrude.

Want to look taller? Devore added the illusion of two or three inches to Raf Vallone's approximately 5-feet-7inch height when he dressed the Italian star for the part of Jean Harlow's stepfather, Marino Bello, in **Harlow**. Devore also made him look slimmer, though his hips tend to be broad.

Here are Devore's rules for adding height ot your appearance. Don't accentuate your shoulders in the hope it will minimize your hips. It is better to match your shoulders to your hips. Then have the bottom of your coat rounded off in front to show as much of your legs as possible. The more leg shown, the taller the effect Jerry Lewis, who is six feet tall, looks even taller because he wears a very short coat and slim pants.

Do you have broad, square shoulders? Don't wear padding; insist on a sloping natural look. Dean Martin's broad shoulders don't look muscle-bound because Devore has all the padding taken out of martin's coats and even has them pinched in slightly at the waist.

Head too small for your shoulders? Remove all padding from the shoulders to give them a sloping look. Aim for slimness in the shoulders to match the head size.

Heavy thighs? Don't wear tight trousers. According to Devore, few men look good in them anyway. This was Sammy Davis' problem before Devore lengthened Davis' very short coats about three quarters of an inch and loosened his skinny pants. Sammy is so pleased with the results that he orders five or six suits at a time.

Big chest? Devore camouflages Richard Burton's massive chest with extra breadth in the front of his coat so that it will hang more easily without broadening his already broad shoulders.

Heavy neck? Dean Martin camouflages his by wearing the collar of his shirts higher in back, but sloping down in front.

Long slim neck? Jerry Lewis wears very high collars to offset it.

Heavy neck or face? No matter how much you like them, bow ties are not for you.

Very thin? Avoid string ties. They'll just make you look forlornly skinny.

There's a knack for camouflaging almost any figure defect. If you have problems not mentioned here, discuss them with a competent tailor. You'll find him ready to cooperate in improving the outer image you present to the world.

ATTITUDE

After you've done everything possible to camouflage a fault of face or figure; take the next step. **Forget it.**

Pamela Tiffin, film star and formerly New York's highest paid high-fashion model, gives this sound advice. "Many professional actors are just as fearful as complete amateurs about revealing their physical shortcomings. What they don't realize is that this very act of trying to keep things concealed reveals them. Concentrate on your good points instead."

Try it. By concentrating on good qualities you'll have no room left for fretting about imperfections. You can't think of two things at the same time.

You might adopt Elke sommer's healthy attitude toward physical blemishes Elke went to a boy's school where she had to be as rough-and-tumble as her masculine classmates. In the process she acquired a number of scars and permanent blemishes, prominent among which is a badly chipped tooth.

Elke ignores the chipped tooth, wearing a cap on it only for film closeups.

"I'm not conscious when I smile that I have a small hole here in my teeth," she told us. "I think that the little imperfections we all have just make us more like able to others if we forget about them."

WHAT IF YOU'RE REALLY HOMELY?

Suppose you're just a homely person, without any particular blemish or major defect that calls for plastic surgery or corrective makeup. What can you do for yourself?

Karl Malden solved the problem when he was a young man. He wanted to act more than anything else in the world, but it was at a time when actors were chosen only from among handsome men.

"I took stock of my appearance," he told us. "I looked in the mirror and made an honest appraisal. I went over the whole thing. I had eyes that were too small and a nose that was too big. How could I ever expect to get leading or important parts with a mug like that?

"I said to myself, 'This is all I've got. I can't change it. So do I want to go ahead and see what I can do with it, or do I want to forget an acting career altogether?'

"I gave an honest answer to that question. I wanted to be an actor."

His decision made Malden face up to the fact that though there were physical attributes he couldn't change, there were things in his personality he could develop., and he set to work on them. Today, few ε k whether Mr. Malden is homely or not, for he radiates an appealing presence that has made him one of the foremost screen actors.

Another great actress on the stage of life, the late Mrs. Eleanor Rossevelt, was confronted with a similar problem. She led a shy childhood because she felt homely and unwanted. One day she realized that she would have to develop her personality to offset her appearance.

Mrs. Roosevelt worked hard on that inner self. With the result that she came to be regarded as a beautiful woman in the true sense of the word.

RADIATE YOUR SELF

We have suggested in an earlier chapter how to use Chekhov's method of radiation to develop worthwhile qualities. Now try using it to radiate your inner self, the self with whom you have been coming closer contact.

Many of us use this method intuitively. The singer who expressess his vibrant self in his song soars to heights of popularity, while another with a much finer voice can't get off the ground.

In his search for star material, talent scout Solly Baiano can easily pick out those who give the self expression. They aren't always handsome young men or beautiful girls, but they all emanate a certain vibrant quality.

You can learn to emanate that quality by aligning your conscious ego with the vibrant self within you. That self never deals in negatives. It is above pattiness in thought or emotion. It doesn't groan and complain under outward conditons. It makes its own conditions in the spirit. It has the supreme confidence necessary to bring those conditions to fruition in the physical world. It is always the master and never the slave.

Practice radiating this self outward. See your physical body surrounded by it as though by an aura of glowing light.

The more strongly you concentrate on that self, the more it will impregnate your whole being. And don't confine the operation of that self to your dealings with the public or to the business world. Make it your vibrant spokesman in all your private affairs and intimate relationships as well.

Whatever your outward appearance may be, that self can transform it into a dynamic presence that will enable you to play a vital role in life rather than halting and self-conscious one.

fifteen

The Unconscious

THE UNCONSCIOUS, YOUR SUBMERGED TREASUREHOUSE

THE unconscious is so vast a subject that one could scarcely touch upon it in a hundred books, let alone one brief chapter. But it must be dealt with, however briefly, since it plays such an important part in helping us give an inspiring performance on the stage of life.

What exactly is the unconscious? According to the dictionary definition it is "that great part of the individual psyche which is inaccessible to consciousness ..."

Dr. Carl G. Jung divided this unconscious into two levels. He termed the level closest to consciousness, the personal unconscious. It contains all the individual experiences, feelings, thoughts and impressions which have ever come to us and which, for one reason or another, have been dismissed from our conscious mind.

In the early days of modern psychology it was believed this was all there was to the unconscious. But after some sixty years of extensive study and psychotherapy, Dr. Jung came to the conclusion that below this personal level exists a vast collective unconscious. He was convinced this unconscious contains all the wisdom gleaned by man during his long sojourn on earth from the very earliest times to the present. Like a great fruitful sea, it lies beneath our conscious endeavor. And by persistent effort we can draw up from it sustenance and help for our daily living.

It can provide us with solutions to the problems which stump or conscious minds. With its aid we can expand our roles and enjoy life more fully. We have only to establish rapport with it to have its valuable treasures at our disposal.

AN ACTOR AND HIS UNCONSCIOUS

The professional actor soon realizes that he **must** have the cooperation of the unconscious if he wants to put on a truly inspired performance. He needs its help to get into the feel of his role. He also needs it to help him experience emotionally the theme of the play so that he can get the dramatist's message across to the audience.

It is on the unconscious he must depend to help him solve problems of performance and troublesome scenes. Most of all, he must have its cooperation in overcoming the deadening routine of night-after-night acting.

However, it is often hard to bring the treasures of the unconscious to the surface. and certainly it can't be done with only a word of command from the conscious mind. Men like Chekhov and Stanislavski developed special methods to help their pupils make contact with their submerged treasure-trove.

STANISLAVSKI'S PRESCRIPTION

In studying means to remedy stereotyped performance Stanislavski found out that routine acting bored the unconscious. A bored unconscious does not bother to contribute anything conscious endeavor. It just falls asleep. This sets up vicious cycle. How to break that cycle?

Stanislavski discovered it could be done if the actor introduced some slight but novel change into his nightly routine. It did not have to be more than a different inflection of the voice in a familiar passage, or a fresh movement of the body.

No matter how insignificant the change was in itself, it had the power to jolt the unconscious awake. And a fully roused and enthusiastic unconscious could be counted on to spill its creativity into the rest of the actor's performance.

TRY THE JOLT METHOD

You might try Stanislavski's method in the everyday of your life.

Deliberately break your humdrum routines by finding ways in which to do your work differently. Don't look for big things to change. Just a little fillip to the unconscious will do the trick. One small change has the power to bring in its wake a train of fresh ideas.

Here, however, is a word of warning. When the ideas come, don't allow inertia to keep you from developing them. You must demonstrate as an actor, not just acknowledge as a passive spectator. Otherwise your unconscious will give you up as a poor investment and go back to sleep again.

PLUMB THE DEEPER WATERS

Once you realize how little it takes to trigger your unconscious into creative action, do take the next step to bring yourself into closer contact with it. This will enable you to call upon it for help in solving problems or developing talents.

There is one important rule for approaching your unconscious . You must be relaxed. Tension shuts the door tightly between you and the unconscious. But relaxation doesn't mean inertia in the mental state any more than it does in the physical. Here, too, true relaxation is a balanced tension between the conscious and unconscious mind.

The best time of day to find this state of balanced tension is in the period of drowsiness that just precedes sleep. Then the conscious mind is loosening its hold, and the unconscious, which is lord of sleep, is beginning to take over. This state can be induced any number of times throughout the day if you wish to accelerate results.

The late Dr. Margaret Steger described this period as the hypnoidal state, and through successful treatment of her patients while they were in it, she proved its enormous therapeutic powers. She took great care, however, to point out that despite the similarity between the terms hypnoidal state and hypnosis proper, they are, in fact, altogether different conditions of being.

The hypnoidal state is that period of deep drowsiness that we all experience just before falling asleep or awakening or in periods of complete relaxation. It is therefore a perfectly normal occurrence in our lives. Hypnosis, on the other hand, is an induced, and therefore artificial state. If wrongfully used it can cause great damage to the psyche, and so should be limited to expert therapists in the field.

Dr. Steger was emphatic in cautioning the layman not to dabble with hypnosis proper either in reference to himself or others. In her book, **Sleep— Your silent Partner in Mental Health**, published by Thomas Nelson in 1961, she differentiated the effects of the two conditions in the following statements:

"A subject in hypnosis has no option but to obey the hypnotic suggestions being imposed on him."

While on the contrary:

"Hypnoidal suggestions can never be imposed on an individual; they will never mislead or deceive."

One can therefore follow the hypnoidal method without fear of self-damage. It is merely the giving of auto-suggestions to the unconscious as we draw in closer contact to it during that normal period of drowsiness which just precedes sleep proper.

RULES FOR CONTACTING THE UNCONSCIOUS IN THE HYPNOIDAL STATE

We follow with some rules to help you establish contact with the unconscious while in the hypnoidal state.

1. When you first go to bed, clear the way for the coming contact by practicing the neutralization of emotion exercise which we have described in Chapter 6. "Emotion." Concentrate on some simple but pleasant occupation until you have worked yourself so completely into the feel of it that you have eliminated all undercurrents of anger, depression or anxiety. This is important because if these strong undercurrents are merely repressed, they will contaminate the hypnoidal state with their negativism.

2. When you feel completely neutralized, bring forward the problem you want to solve. State it aloud, coolly and factually. giving a broad outline of it together with pertinent details. Explain to your unconscious why you need help, telling your story as though you were speaking to a very wise and powerful counselor. Don't try to solve anything yourself.

3. Once you have stated your problem, prepare to turn it over to your unconscious. Your words might run something like this:

"You know the problem. I am trusting it to you. I know you will give me the best solution."

You may prefer other words to express your needs more fully. But be careful in the words you select. Any negative is passed over by your unconscious. So if you say, "I am not worrying about it any more," the unconscious will simply skip the 'not' and you will be firmly planting a worry thought in your mind.

4. When you have formulated your request, repeat it over and over to your unconscious in a confident but soothing rhythmical monotone. Monotony, combined with rhythm, gives what you are saying and added impetus. It also induces the hypnoidal state which is so necessary to this method.

5. If you fall asleep during your recitation, well and good. Otherwise, complete this little exercise by making a conscious act of letting both your problem and your request for help drop into your unconscious.

Problem will not be solved all at once by this method. The unconscious can't be hurried into delivering up its secrets. But rely on the knowledge that if you maintain your relaxation and your confidence it **will** answer you.

The answers will come in surprising ways. Perhaps you will wake up one morning to find a solution to your problem already worked out by your own mind while you slept. Perhaps you will be led to consult with someone who can help you, or you will come upon a book that will show you the way. Perhaps you will feel simply a new fount of strength and patience opening up within to tide you over a difficult time.

But whatever may be the answer to your particular problem, you'll be surprised at the depth of understanding it brings, and the wise solution it presents to your conscious mind.

AN ADDED HELP—THE SYLLOGISM

Sometimes you may find that results are not forthcoming, despite all your efforts. If this happens, examine the form of address you are using to see if you've allowed fuzziness to creep into your plea. Psychology books tell you that the unconscious is always a willing friend and servant, but only if you approach it in the forms it understands.

The unconscious works from deductive reasoning. Therefore the most potent suggestions you can give it are in the language of the simple but absolute syllogism. Why? Because a syllogism is a perfect example of concise deductive reasoning carried from its opening premise to its conclusion.

What exactly is a syllogism? It is a statement followed by a qualification which can be interpreted finally in only one way. This three-part presentation provides the unconscious with a graphic road map that it cannot fail to understand.

The writers have found it effective where other methods have failed. So if you are having trouble making contact, try the syllogistic form of address. Be sure it's a perfect syllogism, however, with every part ringing true. For example: Suppose you are searching for your calling in life. You're bewildered and uncertain, wondering if you do have talent.

The following syllogism will help you, first to regain your badly shaken faith in yourself, and secondly to orient your unconscious mind to the problem.

1. Every human being possesses a talent of some sort.
2. I am a human being.
3. Therefore, I have a talent.

You can utter this syllogism with perfect faith because it presents a simple truth. Repeat it throughout the day, and especially in the hypnoidal state before you fall asleep.

It works. Suddenly doors will begin to open for you. You will find yourself thinking more clearly of projects you are interested in. You will be led in one direction or another. And finally your talent will stand revealed to you.

At the first sign of this talent, which may be an insistent inclination to write, a second syllogims may be devised to help strengthen it. For Example:

1. All things manifest after their kind
2. My kind is to manifest by writing
3. Therefore I must write to manifest

Syllogisms may be used in a variety of ways—to reenforce one's self-confidence, to emphasize a quality one wishes to cultivate, or to locate some hidden talent or skill.

CHEKHOV'S CENTER

Michael Chekhov used to teach his pupils that each one possessed an interior aide. If they could make contact with this aide he or she would lead them into a deeper and more vibrant way of playing their parts on the state of life, as well as the theater. He called this aide the Center.

To make it simpler to understand, Chekhov suggested that the students regard themselves as actually three person. One, the physical person who performed the action. Two, the mental person who observed the action. Three, the spiritual person who Supervised and coordinated the mental and physical personalities.

Our mental and physical selves, Chekhov pointed out, lead cramped and selfish lives. But the spiritual self sees wide horizons and experiences sublime emotions.

This is because the spiritual self is the eternal part of each of us. It revolves around the Center of our being. and that Center is the channel through which all great creative impulses flow to us.

If you have been practicing some of the preceding exercises in this book the Center will have already begun to take form for you. Now practice evoking it consciously. Remember that the unconscious has no power to grasp abstract ideas, so you must present it with a vivid picture.

Imagine the Center as a superhuman presence, all powerful, wise and good. See it standing by your side. a ready counselor. Firmly believe that every time you ask for advice or help, it will respond.

IN TIMES OF CRISIS

At such times the sense of our own inadequacy often paralyzes our thinking. We find ourselves longing to place our problem in the hands of someone strong and wise enough to take care of us.

Now, tell yourself that it is not necessary for you to handle this crisis alone. The Center will help you.

Next, evoke your pictorial representation of the Center. See that superhuman presence standing at your shoulder prepared to guide you through the crisis. Concentrate on that image until it becomes real to you.

Be sure it has the vitality of life. Don't let it remain static. Make it move to the right of you, then to the left of you, in front of you and behind you. Encourage it even to fly above your head like a guardian angel.

Begin to converse aloud with it. Tell it about your problem. Go into details. Finally ask it to flow back into your body and take over for you. Feel its clear cool rhythms surging through you. See them surrounding you in a calm deep aura of light

Once you feel yourself filled with this superhuman presence turn your crisis over to its keeping. Then relax in the belief that everything will be properly handled.

"Relaxation is a decision in itself," Carry Grants points out. "You have a choice whether or not to relax. To do nothing-that in itself is a decision. Tell yourself God will take care of your problem. God is the center of yourself."

WHEN GRIEF COMES

Sometimes we are called upon to give comfort to friends, relatives or members of our immediate family who are suffering from the loss of a dear one. The only comfort our mental self can conjure up often expresses itself in stereotyped expressions of condolence that fall far short of the mark. How inadequate we feel at those times! How we long to give the real comfort that is so sorely needed!

If you are confronted with this cruel chore, learn to rely of the Center to guide your tongue. See it as a compassionate presence standing at your side. Give that presence strength and vitality by dwelling upon it. Then ask it to fill your body and speak the necessary words of comfort through your lips.

Thus you will find it possible to help those who stand in such great need.

IF THE LOSS IS YOURS

In the aftermath of such a shock, life often seems scarcely worth living. We tend to withdraw into the cave of bleak despair. In that cave nothing splendid or creative can happen.

Perhaps you have suffered a loss so devastating that you cannot bear to face life. Try calling on the Center to help you return to the world and take up your share of duties and responsibilities again.

See the Center as a strong, self-confident presence with shoulders broad enough to bear the weight of grief which is crushing you. Then permit it to flow through your whole body, lending you its strength and calm. Use that reservoir to do your daily chores.

Whenever you find yourself tending to withdraw from the world, renew your close communion with that Center. Consciously turn over it to again the duties which your mental self finds almost impossible to perform.

It may be hard at first to relinquish your grief and force yourself back into patterns of living. But if you do, you will find that gradually your sorrow will subside. Eventually it will reach proportions easier to bear.

You may even discover yourself in possession of an answer to the why of things that will broaden and enrich your whole life.

DON'T WAIT FOR CRISIS

But why wait for a crisis to put yourself on close terms with the Center? Learn to call upon it to help you solve the minor irritations of everyday living. Align yourself closely with it in your workaday world.

It will revitalize your life in undreamed of ways and make every day joyful and creative experience. And when a major crisis strikes, that Center will be with you so that you will not have to grope blindly to search it out.

sixteen

Your Life Drama

SUPEROBJECTIVE

TO BE a success every piece of drama must possess a clearcut superobjective. The superobjective is the end toward which the play moves, as well as the guiding force that gives meaning to each act. Without such a superobjective the play world be only a loosely knit series of unrelated and confusing actions meandering over the stage.

How about the superobjective in the play of your life? Have you a clearcut one? Or is your drama made up of an assortment of uncorrelated and aimless deeds in which your superobjective lies buried unrecognized?.

"I UNDERSTAND IT, BUT I DON'T LIKE IT"

Director Daniel Man told us this story about Boris Aronson, designer for many New York stage hits, whom he met at the opening of a recent play. After the first act Mann asked Aronson his opinion.

"I love it, but I don't understand it," Aronson replied. After the second act Mann asked Aronson if he was still as enthusiastic.

To which Aronson replied, "I understand it now, but I don't like it."

Is your life drama expressed in this little story? Look back on your childhood. You did not understand what the play of your life was all about then, but you loved every minute of it. This was because you were in tune with your superobjective.

Now, as you have grown older, do you still greet each moment with the same enthusiasm of your childhood, or do you feel that you understand life completely now and you don't like it? Perhaps you need to take a long look at your superobjective. The cause of jaded or depressed living always lies with a faulty superobjective.

ARE YOU ACCEPTING A LIMITING SUPER OBJECTIVE FROM CHILDHOOD

Unhappy childhood experiences have the power, if we let them to saddle us with limiting negative superobjectives. Sometimes these take the form of crushing defeatism-- "Nothing I do ever turns out right. "Sometimes they're nothing more elevating than an obsession to "get even," to "show them all." Even if such a superobjective has the power to carry us far in worldly success, it will never bring peace of mind.

Here is an interesting truth. Whatever your childhood experience may have been, you don't need to cling to the limiting superobjectives they have bequeathed to you.

Vera Miles, the lovely and talented screen and television star, was a child of the Depression, living in the direst kind of poverty. Her parents were divorced when she was small, and she hardly knew her father. Her more fortunate schoolmates in the little town of Pratt, Kansas, ostracized her because she came from "the wrong side of the tracks."

Vera Miles have adopted a defeatist or vengeful superobjective. She chose, instead, to take a constructive view of her childhood misfortunes.

"I have a very deep-seated feeling, call it religion if you wish," she told us, "that if you can learn to accept everything that happens to you as something that is best for you, it will make you grow into a bigger and better person and you can't help profiting from it".

Whenever Vera's childhood classmates who snubbed her write her fan letters, she takes special pains to answer them graciously.

"It's really hard work to be bitter continually," she told us out of her deep insight. "And I'm not that ambitious."

Have you been working hard to maintain a negative superobjective of your own? If so., why not turn it in for a more expansive and creative one? You will experience a renewal of meaning and interest in your life. For an expansive superobjective tends to freedom just as a negative one does to bondage.

MATERIAL SUPEROBJECTIVES

Is your superobjective, on the other hand, just a material one concerned only with attaining a position of power or amassing a million dollars?

There is nothing wrong with obtaining material advantages. Life is meant to bring us abundances. But man cannot limit himself to the acquisition of material goods and still be happy. Today he has progressed so far along in civilization that he can invent machines capable of "thinking money"!

In a speech before the AFL-CIO Convention in November of 1963, Secretary of Labor Willard Wirtz explained the situation in these words: "What has happened is that technology has now developed to the point where machines have' on the average' ability equivalent to a high school education. More precisely; most work which has been done by people with less than a high school education can now be done more cheaply by machines."

To keep ahead of the very machines we have created, we must move on to more lofty superobjectives to satisfy our deepest needs.

IS A CAREER A FITTING OBIECTIVE?

A career is a fine goal. but it is an inadequate superobjective. This has been proved in the lives of individuals who have dedicated themselves solely to their careers, only to feel frustrated and unhappy.

When beautiful Inger Stevens began her acting career she devoted all her energies to achieving success in it. This was her sole superobjective.

Then something happened to Inger's personal affairs that shattered her self-confidence. The superobjective that she had made of her career had no sustaining power on which she could rely. Inger found herself lost in a blind alley of hopelessness. One day she took a handful of sleeping pills.

For three days she lay unconscious in her room. For nine more days and nights she was in a coma in the hospital. She come out of the coma to find herself with an uphill fight to regain her health. She had a blood clot on one lung and the acid in the drug she had taken had blinded her.

For three months she lived in a state of complete despair. The superobjective was shattered by her blindness. She saw life as a vacant road stretching out before her. She could not bear to face it, and lived her days as a recluse.

Finally at the urging of her psychiatrist, she agreed to make her first contact with the outside world by accompanying him to a performance of **Carmen** at the Metropolitan Opera House. Everything swam about her in a blur of vague and formless color. For a moment, seated in that dark house, staring at the blurred stage, she was seized by panic. This, she told herself, was all life would ever hold for her again.

Then a miraculous thing happened to Inger Stevens That moment of panic was followed by a complete revelation. Inger faced herself for the first time in her life.

"I suddenly realized," she told us, "that all through my career I had just been playing one role after the other, that I had been living in my roles alone. I made up my mind that it was not my career but life itself that was important, and that from them on I would live it as best I could and accept all its challenges, even my blindness to begin with, and turn them to advantage."

With this new superobjective, Inger found the courage to climb out of her former restricted way of thinking into a new life. Healing forces were released. Gradually her sight came back. Once again she was free to resume her career. But there was a difference.

She told us about it. "After having once tried deliberately to do away with life, I find my greatest joy in learning to appreciate living for its own sake".

WHAT CONSTITUTES A VITAL SUPEROBJECTVE

The creative quality of living for its own sake must animate every vital superobjective. Far from replacing the goals of the physical and mental selves, this vibrant quality should enhance them and make them more meaningful. And they in turn **must** serve the deeper requirements of the superobjective to bring satisfaction into your life.

The late Edmund Gwenn, the magnificent old actor who starred in **Miracle on 34th street**, translated the talent for humor which made him famous as a comedian into the realm of his superobjective. According to his friends, even when he was suffering his last illness he did not allow carping or morbidity to intrude in his conversations with them.

Director George Seaton recalled the many long talks he had with the 82-year-old actor, bedridden in the Motion Picture Country Home. He would find Gwenn bristling with various tubes which had been inserted into his body to keep him alive. But Gwenn never discussed those tubes. Instead, his conversations with Seaton revolved around the difficulty of playing comedy on stage in comparison to tragedy.

"All the honors go to the tragedian for chewing up the scenery," Gwenn joked. "While the comedian, who has to be much more subtle to be funny, is just loudly criticized when he doesn't come through."

He and Seaton marveled often about this idiosyncracy of human nature that invariably rated gloomy performances above merry ones.

One day Seaton, coming into the room and looking down at his game old friend, felt a sudden surge of compassion.

"All this must be terribly difficult for you, Teddy," he said sympathetically.

Gwenn didn't buy that sympathy. A smile touched his lips.

"Not nearly as difficult as playing comedy," he answered cheerfully.

They were his words of exit. His head turned on the pillow. He was dead. Up to his last breath and in spite of great physical suffering, Gwenn had actually lived the gentle whimsicality on which his career was based.

HOW TO DISCOVER YOUR SUPEROBJECTIVE

You, too, can live a rich, satisfying life by the light of a creative superobjective, one to which you can give your full allegiance as the theme of your life play. Bob Gist suggests the following method to his students to help them find themselves.

Set a time to be apart from others Relax. Then ask yourself this question:

"Who am I?"

Don't let the mask you're wearing give you a glib answer. Push it aside and listen to the spiritual self deep within you. It's been buried and deprived of a voice for so long that you may not hear its reply all at once.

But don't stop. Begin to ask related questions of yourself. Questions like, "What do I need of life?" "What are my goals?" "What do I desire for myself?" "What do I really expect to accomplish?" "What do I really want to be?"

Sooner or later, if you continue to push aside trivial explanations you will begin to get different and exciting answers. When they come, jot them down along with the thoughts that circle them. At first you may sound vague and indefinite to yourself. It's obvious you've never taken the trouble to become acquainted with **you.** Don't despair. Take a little time each day to get together with yourself and ask more questions. Make a diary of your daily answers and look them over now and then. Gradually the fog will start lifting. You will begin to see more clearly what you expect of life, what you would like to contribute to life, and eventually you will find yourself with your real superobjective.

SOME DO'S AND DON'TS

In determining your superobjective, don't be guided by small, easily attainable dreams. A superobjective that can be easily attained will never satisfy that deepest self. A superobjective should be a light leading you on, not a possession to be packed safely away in a trunk in the attic of your mind.

Jemes Coburn told us Stella Adler always advises her pupils, "Genius is in your choice."

This means simply that you have it within your power to choose a creative superobjective, for there is in everyone of us a genius for life and more life. It is up to us whether or not to give it expression.

Your superobjective must include concern both for your self and your fellow man, whatever his race, creed or color. It must concern itself with life in general. This concern and communion with all life is as basic a need of your spiritual self as food and drink are to your physical self.

Your superobjective cannot be governed by expediency. If you voice convictions to which you don't fully subscribe yourself, but which are merely a product of teaching or environment, you will not have uncovered your true superobjective. The spiritual self starves on mimicry,and you will be playing your role in life in a hollow and unconvincing manner.

Daniel Mann told us that the same holds true for stage actors who ask themselves how they should be feeling in a given situation instead of concentrating on living that situation.

"The personal essence of man or a woman can come through only when a person is completely involved in the right way." he explained. "The wrong way is the anticipation of how one should feel and then "feeling" that way. So work for results. Don't just try to show them.

"It's like eating. The body takes over the digesting. You simply put the food in your mouth."

DON'T JUST TALK IDEALS

When you have formulated your superobjective clearly follow this motto to the best of your ability: "Don't talk ideals. Live them."

It is easy to pay lip service to our high ideals while giving them no place in our lives. To keep yourself within the bounds of integrity, try expressing your superojective through deeds alone. If you cannot express it with deeds but must rely on your tongue, your superobjective is not operating in your life.

Don't let your superobjective go into hiding when times get rough. Then is when you should express yourself most clearly and decisively.

"Being dedicated brings out the best in man, whether on the stage of life or the theater, " Mann said. "And if you will notice, it is people who are dedicated who are usually the quietest people. They don't need to assert themselves. They have faith in their superobjective even to staking their lives on it. With faith like that you don't have to talk."

THE THROUGHGOING ACTION

Once a dramatist defines his superobjective a theme, he is ready to begin constructing his play. A good dramatist builds that play by using a series of lesser objectives. Each one of these, when accomplished, leads the characters in the play a step nearer the superobjective which can be finally realized only as the curtain goes down.

Stanislavski called the forward movement of the objectives toward the realization of the superobjective, the "throughgoing action." Any play in which the "throughgoing action" splinters in all directions instead of traveling in a straight line toward the superobjective cannot be successful. If players and directors wish to make something of such a play they must reorientate the action provide that unity of purpose which "throughgoing action" presupposes.

THE THROUGHGOING ACTION IN YOUR OWN LIFE

Look at the happenings of your daily living. Do they form a purposeful arrow formation toward your superobjective, or do they form a jumble of undirected movements that spray out everywhere? Stanislavski described this condition in a play in terms of a beautiful statue which has been splintered into many pieces. That disarray of bits and scraps will scarcely revealed the loveliness of the unbroken statue, no matter how hard you stare at it.

A PLAN FOR DEVELOPMENT

Splintered "throughgoing action" usually comes from seeing our superobjective only in wide general terms. It floats like a nimbus around our heads instead of being drawn concretely into our lives.

Laura Huxley prescribes the following method to help her patients realize both objectives and superobjectives in everyday giving.

1. Decide upon an immediate objective. Set a time limit to the accomplishment of that objective. Ask yourself what you would like to have make of your life three years from now, or if you prefer an even shorter limit, one year from now.

But in setting upon this objective. Mrs. Huxley gives this warning: "You must take care that your objective is not in opposition to your real self, because this will cause you to dissipate your energy in the ensuing discomfort."

2. Once you have set a time limit and an immediate goal, ask yourself how you will look when you have reached it. Will

you be more poised and self-confident? Will you be more successful materially? Will your career have been furthered? Will you have grown appreciably toward a fuller development of the inner self?

Provide yourself with a vivid picture of how you will appear by the end of that time, if you have reached your goal. This will present your unconscious both with a blueprint to follow and a stimulant to urge it on.

3.Maintain a straight "throughgoing action" to this objective: But check on yourself now and then, as stage actors do during the course of a play, to see if you are still on the beam of the superobjective. It is so easy to stray and create splintered ineffectual action patterns unless you make these periodic self checkups.

A METHOD OF BRINGING YOURSELF INTO CONTACT WTIH THE VITALITY A TRUE SUPER OBJECTIVE CONTAIINS

One sure symptom of being out of key with your superobjective is a sense of boredom a depression. A true superobjective keeps you in warm, enthusiastic rapport with life.

When you suffer such spells, try the following little exercise Lajos Egri suggests. He practices it himself now and then when he finds the edges of his enthusiasm for life are dulling. He related the following story to show that his simple formula works, not only far himself, but for others.

One day a young girl phoned to tell him she was tired of life and meant to commit suicide.

"Try this first, "Mr. Egri told her. " Blindfold yourself for twenty-four hours, and after that if you still wish to commit suicide I will not try to dissuade you."

The girl agreed to the curious request and hung up. Mr. Egri didn't hear from her for seven months. Then he received a letter from her. Twenty –four hours of living with the handicap of blindness, she told him, had not only cured her of the idea of suicide but had released tremendous positive forces within her. She was now happily married and expecting a baby.

For an hour or two, try depriving yourself of one of the gifts nature bestowed on you. For instance, blindfold yourself and see what it is like to grope your way in blankness. Or deliberately deprive yourself of the use of a let or an arm. Through the use of your imagination simulate any handicap you choose.

When the time is over, a deep gratitude and joy at your own wholeness, a realization of the preciousness of Life, will have replaced the former feeling of boredom and depression. And you will be able to align yourself again with your superobjective, the very core of life.

A TRUE SUPEROBJECTIVE EXPANDS

After you have attained your first objective, set yourself a fresh one, again with a time limit. Keep up this progressive series of objectives for yourself just as a dramatist does, but be sure that each fresh objective still leads you to the superobjective that you have accepted as your guiding light.

If that superobjective is a true one you will never be able to overtake it. But as you seem to approach it, it will reveal ever more stimulating adventures for you to fashion into the rich well rounded drama you are making of your life.